Praise for *NEW YORK MINUTE*

"*New York Minute*, Laurence Overmire's latest collection of poetry, brilliantly expresses the exhilaration, fear, heartache, joy, disappointment, laughter and, ultimately, the loss of innocence that actors undergo when moving to New York to embark on a life in the theatre."
  Dea Lawrence, *CMO, Variety*

"I just have finished Laurence Overmire's *New York Minute*, and I have fallen in love with his memories. This book, a memoir-in-poetry of his years as an actor in and out of New York, will be invaluable to aspiring actors looking forward, and actors emeritus, ready to look back. It's as if Overmire's personal history has dissolved into words, dissolved further into feeling, dissolved finally into truth."
  Margie Boulé, *Actress/Singer/Writer/Journalist*

"Laurence's poetry crafts scenes as vivid as any painter. The individual poems are stirring views of real life as seen through the eyes and experiences of the poet. The collected works represent a journey anyone can relate to. Perfect reading while on a plane!"
  Paul T. Couch, *VP, Gary Musick Productions,*
  former Director of Entertainment, Dollywood

"My thanks to Laurence Overmire for writing this poetic guide for his fellow travelers. It is a helpful meditation for those with a New York minute in their past, their future, or who, like me, might be in the midst of one right now."
  The Rev. Dr. William Lupfer, *Rector,*
  Trinity Church Wall Street

"Rediscover New York as never before, and let yourself be carried away by the wonderful poems of Laurence Overmire, who opens our minds and hearts to our humanity. Always in search of this warm union between humans, so dear to his heart, he offers the best of himself, by encouraging us to encounter the dynamism of this city, and the love and compassion he carries for these inhabitants. Once you go through the doors of *New York Minute*, you will never be the same again."
  Jacques Macaire, Founder and Director,
  HUMANBE, Paris, France

NEW YORK MINUTE

An Actor's Memoir

Laurence Overmire

 INDELIBLE MARK PUBLISHING

Indelible Mark Publishing 2017

Copyright 2017 by Laurence Overmire.

All rights reserved. This book, or any part thereof, may not be reproduced in any form without permission, except in the case of brief quotations embodied in critical articles and reviews.

Editing, cover/interior design, back cover author photo: Nancy McDonald

Interior photos from the personal collection of Laurence Overmire

Front cover photo:
View of New York skyline, Brooklyn Bridge over the East River and tugboat in fog, NY by Joseph Sohm/Shutterstock

Back cover photo:
Statue of Liberty and the New York City Skyline by Sean Pavone/Shutterstock

Library of Congress Control Number 2017945968

ISBN 978-0-9795398-8-6

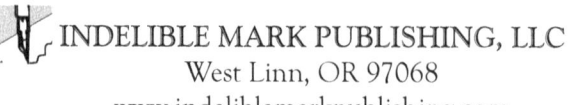

INDELIBLE MARK PUBLISHING, LLC
West Linn, OR 97068
www.indeliblemarkpublishing.com

For my good friends and fellow thespians
Russell Leib, Dorian Gray Ross & Richert Easley
who, during my time in New York, were a source of
strength, intelligence, wit and encouragement

Books of poetry by Laurence Overmire

- The Ghost of Rabbie Burns
  An American Poet's Journey Through Scotland
- Gone Hollywood
- Report From X-Star 10
  Sci-Fi Poetry
- Honor & Remembrance
  A Poetic Journey through American History

More books by Laurence Overmire

- Digging for Ancestral Gold
  The Fun and Easy Way to Get Started on Your Genealogy Quest
- The One Idea That Saves the World
  A Call to Conscience and A Call to Action
- One Immigrant's Legacy
  The Overmyer Family in America, 1751-2009
- A Revolutionary American Family
  The McDonalds of Somerset County, New Jersey
- William R. McDonald and Abigail Fowler of Herkimer County, New York and Their Descendants
- The McDonalds of Lansingburgh, Rensselaer County, New York
  The Pioneering Family of Richard and Catharine (Lansing) McDonald and Their Descendants

Videopoems by Laurence Overmire on YouTube

- Ode to an Endangered Species
- Maybe the Trees
- Viewpoint
- Beach Walk at Sunset

TABLE OF CONTENTS

FOREWORD	i
PREFACE	v
TAKING MANHATTAN	
Crossing the Hudson*	3
When First You See New York	5
This One Place	7
Through the Back Door*	10
How You Hold Your Fork*	13
Peeking Behind Door Number 2	15
The Algonquin Square Table*	16
An Actor Prepared*	17
Amadeus*	18
The Broadhurst Theatre*	19
Mozart*	21
Still Life*	22
Why Can't You?*	24
From the Top*	25
The Dancer	26
Ghosts on Broadway	27
Washington Square Park in Fall*	28
Strawberry Fields	30
Lost Masterpiece*	32
Lady in the Window	33

* See Liner Notes for more background on these poems

Diablerie	34
East Side Ladies	35
While Strolling Down Fifth Avenue	36
Watch Winding	37

BRIDGING BROOKLYN

Brooklyn Bridge*	41
The Balloon*	42
Field of Lost Dreams	43
Look Homeward, Angel	46
Brooklyn Rhapsody*	48
Something About the Hat	51
The Winter of '83	52
Nailed: The Aftermath of a Bad Audition*	54
Prepared for the Worst	55
It's Only Business*	56
Seafood Stew	57
Stage Kiss	58
Priceless Mementos*	59
Add and Subtract	60
The Woman in Black	61
The Comfort of Strangers	62
Saturday Night	63
New York Deli	64
Coney Island, 1985	66
Hook, Line and Pizza*	68

* See Liner Notes for more background on these poems

The Dude in Leather Jacket	69
Café Around the Corner	70
Manly Man	71
Chances	72
Subway Rider*	74
Brooklyn Nights	76
Words*	77
Kitten*	78
Two Timing	80
Famed*	81
The Day John McEnroe Glared at Me*	82
On the Road*	85
Throwing Tomatoes	86
Man Called Thunder*	87
Hanging with the Devil	88
The Second Coming	89
In Memory Of*	90
War in the Bedroom	91
Ringing	92
Born and Died	93
Victims	94
Curtain Down*	95
Gardens*	96
Two Brothers	97
Old Man and a Bench	100
All the World	101

* See Liner Notes for more background on these poems

LEAVING NEW YORK
Let Be* 105
Buffets and Rewards 106
Newton's Apple 107
Vagabond Shoes* 109
When Sinatra Died* 111
Cake in the Freezer 113

A NEW MILLENNIUM
A Few Short Decades, More* 117
Like Any Other 118
Tower 2, Floor 87* 120
One September Morning 121
Where Have You Gone? 122
Differences 123

RETURN TO NEW YORK
Return* 127
Good Old New York 129
The Corporation* 131
Soiree at the Met* 132
Warholed 133
The Players 134
The New New York 137
Early Morning, Sept. 11, 2011 140
New York Minute 143

* See Liner Notes for more background on these poems

PHOTO ALBUM	149
LINER NOTES	161
ACKNOWLEDGEMENTS	177
AUTHOR BIOGRAPHY	179

FOREWORD

As a longtime follower and fan of Laurence Overmire I was delighted with this new volume of poetry, *New York Minute, An Actor's Memoir*. I had expected to enjoy the collection, I had not expected it to engage me completely and become a new favorite.

One reason for my enchantment, I believe, is because these poems are about his years in New York City. I grew up in another large city and although Chicago may trail the Big Apple in some ways, there are immutable traits shared by large cities. Those traits surfaced in verse after verse of *New York Minute* and I was transported to another time and place in my life – a remarkably pleasant experience.

The magic starts early and by the third poem I was hooked. *This One Place* shines a light on the interdependent relationship of an individual in a large and highly diverse population.

> *People of every out of way place*
> *Of every size and color*
> *Speak a thousand different languages*
> *Trying to find the common bond*
> *That makes us all*
>
> *One*
>
> *You cannot walk these streets*
> *Without confronting some*
> *Heretofore unknown*
> *Unexplored*
> *Aspect of yourself*

Overmire's experience as an actor struggling to make his dream come true is unique to a small share of us, but he voices desires and yearnings common to all; success, happiness, love, a place to belong. We are shown the loneliness of crowds and the frightening darkness of well-lit streets. We experience the loss of people and places and the stealth stalking of a mischievous kitten.

Indeed, the book is for more than actors and those who have experienced life in large busy places. There is the age-old struggle of communication between the sexes in a brief poem called *War in the Bedroom*. *When Sinatra Died* is a tribute not only to the man but the era, and perhaps the mindset he represented. A favorite of mine is *The Algonquin Square Table*:

> *Just let me remind you:*
> *Poetry is not life.*
> *Life is poetry.*

This splendid collection reconfirms my admiration of Mr. Overmire's talents. Many of the poems are witty and amusing while others highlight the inescapable cynicism of our times.

One notable feature of the book, which surprised and delighted me, is a chapter called Liner Notes which offers a brief explanation of the whys and wherefores of many of the pieces. Nice touch!

So as a city girl and part-time poet I recommend *New York Minute* unreservedly, or perhaps I should say in a Chicago Minute, which by my calculations is only seconds behind.

       Jean Sheldon
       Poet, *Persistent* and *Jelly Side Down*
       Author, *The Woman in the Wing,*
       The Nic & Nora Mysteries, et al.

PREFACE

Shortly after graduating from the University of Minnesota with an M.F.A. in acting and having completed a one-year Bush Fellowship as a professional actor at the Guthrie Theatre in Minneapolis, Minnesota, I got married. After a short honeymoon, my wife and I headed to New York City to begin a new life adventure in the spring of 1982. I was 24 years old.

We first stayed in an actor friend's apartment in Washington Heights overlooking the George Washington Bridge and the Hudson River. It was a great view, but the neighborhood outside the back door was part of a very gritty Harlem – a huge change from the comfortable suburban milieu of middle America with which we were accustomed. The incredibly fast pace of the city was exhausting. We would come home after a day of subway riding and collapse. It took our bodies about two weeks to acclimate.

Soon after our Washington Heights experience, we found a sublet on West 76th Street on the Upper West Side.[1] Our place wasn't much bigger than a large closet – there was a mini kitchen, a small fridge and a loft in which to sleep. We loved the neighborhood, but it cost an arm and a leg. Still, we were young and intrepid.

I quickly landed my first acting job in the Big Apple with Joseph Papp's New York Shakespeare Festival in Moliere's *Don Juan*, directed by Richard Foreman and starring John Seitz, Roy Brocksmith and Pamela Payton-Wright. A few other actors in that production scaled the heights to fame: Melissa Leo, Jere Burns and Kelly

---

[1] We rented the place from two actresses who I found out years later were college friends of my second wife, Nancy McDonald. Coincidence?

McGillis.[2] I have very fond memories of strolling a few blocks east to Central Park on many a beautiful summer evening and working at the splendid Delacorte Theatre – in one of the great classics of literature! It doesn't get much better for a young actor than that, especially one newly arrived in the city.

Our rent in Manhattan was prohibitive and our apartment was just too small, so we moved to the more affordable environs of Brooklyn later that summer, first to Boerum Hill and then to Carroll Gardens, an Italian neighborhood just south of Brooklyn Heights. I loved the history of Brooklyn, the stomping grounds of Gen. George Washington and the writer Thomas Wolfe, not to mention the former home of the mythic Boys of Summer, the Brooklyn Dodgers.

At the end of that same momentous summer of '82, I was cast in a Broadway show: Peter Shaffer's *Amadeus* starring Frank Langella, Dennis Boutsikaris and Suzanne Lederer, directed by Sir Peter Hall. Several other stars joined the cast over the course of time: David Dukes, David Birney, Mark Hamill[3] and John Pankow. The show finally closed on Oct. 16, 1983. One of my fellow cast members, Mary Elizabeth Mastrantonio, went on to film stardom in *The Color of Money* (1986), for which she was nominated for an Academy Award.

---

[2] Frank Rich, "Don Juan: Offbeat Moliere in Central Park," New York Times, July 2, 1982.

[3] Mark Hamill was a big celebrity at the time having made his claim to fame in the *Star Wars* films. He and I and several other young male actors would rush offstage after our scenes and gather around a new-fangled computer to play what was at that time a very primitive video game about Dracula. Lacking the graphics and sound effects of modern video games, we had to type in commands and questions to try to hunt down and solve the mystery of the Count of Transylvania. Even then, the game was very addictive.

Being an actor in New York was a dream come true for me. Though opportunities were few (the job market for actors was always depressed), I managed to keep working, landing a job here and a job there, many of them on the road, and supplementing my income with a variety of side jobs – cleaning apartments, doing telemarketing, even driving a horse-drawn carriage in Central Park. The insecurity of the lifestyle took a toll on my marriage. It was always a financial struggle to pursue the dream, but you can't put a price tag on life experience. It was very difficult, but I loved it! Most of my memories are good ones. I was immersed in the daily development of my craft constantly stimulated by the reading of scripts and books in one of the world's greatest and most arts-conscious cities.

Beginning about 1983, I was employed by Simon & Kumin Casting as an actor to read with other actors who were auditioning for various stage and film projects. I was involved in the casting of several Broadway shows including *Brighton Beach Memoirs*, *Biloxi Blues*, *Broadway Bound*, *Sleight of Hand* and *Rags*. I played audition scenes opposite a lot of performers who would later become stars of stage and screen including Viggo Mortensen, Edward Norton, Sarah Jessica Parker, Elizabeth Shue, Patrick Dempsey, James Spader, Michael O'Keefe, Helen Hunt, Christine Lahti and Marisa Tomei. Meanwhile, on the casting side of the table were such notables as Neil Simon, Gene Saks, Gary Sinise, Stephen Schwartz, Charles Strouse, John Guare and many more.

In 1985, I flew to Anchorage, Alaska, to do a production of *Twelfth Night* starring Ethan Phillips and Susan Diol. I not only acted in that show, but also worked as an assistant to the director, Roy Brocksmith. One night during rehearsal, we witnessed an astonishing display of the Northern Lights overhead just outside our rehearsal hall. The experience awakened the poet deep within me. In the days that followed I penned one of my first poems, *Aurora Borealis*. Thereafter, I turned to poetry as a way to document my life's experience, creating what I call a "diary in art." I discovered that by revisiting important events in my poetic imagination, those experiences became more discerningly perceptive and meaningful. The poetry was teaching me things about myself and about life that I had overlooked and had not made conscious.

Several of the poems in this book were among my earliest and were written in the 1980's. My marriage ended in divorce in 1990, amicably so, but I was ready for a complete change of scenery. I moved to Los Angeles in 1991. There I was confronted with the crass commercialization of my beloved art form, experiences and impressions that I recorded poetically in *Gone Hollywood* (2011).

The poems presented here are solidly based in real life experience. Many of the stories are true. Of course, there's a modicum of poetic license in the details, but I have always been interested in getting to the deep truths of real life.

I had no desire to publish these early poems at the time. I wrote most of them for myself, for my own edification, not for any particular audience or publisher. In fact, it wasn't until the late 90's that I made my first attempts to publish my material.

When I left New York, I didn't look back. I was remarried and living in Oregon when 9/11 happened in 2001. I was shocked and heartbroken. Our greatest fears were realized; the hatreds and tensions of the world had been simmering for many, many years, waiting to explode. In the aftermath of that nightmare, I determined, for my own part, to commit my life to creating a sane, healthy and compassionate world.

The new millennium brought about a new burst of New York-themed poetry as I reflected on the city and its meaning to my own life and the world itself.

In 2009, I returned to New York for the first time since I left. It had changed dramatically. Though parts of it were cleaner, particularly around the Times Square/Broadway theatre district, it had lost much of its authenticity. Gone were many of my favorite haunts, the colorful mom and pop stores and local diners, only to be replaced by the usual bland corporate monoliths you see everywhere else in the U.S. and around the world. Is this the future? I hope not.

For all of us, whether we realize it or not, life takes place in a New York minute, in an instant that vanishes into thin air.

As a poet and an artist, I have to believe that New Yorkers will, in the years to come, revive the spirit of innovation and creativity of the world's great gathering place and find new ways to lead us all into what must become, if humankind is to survive, the compassionate heart of the 21st century.

Laurence Overmire
West Linn, Oregon, USA

Taking Manhattan

Crossing the Hudson

The possibility of a New World
Loomed in front of me
As I crossed for the first time
Over the George Washington Bridge

Coming from a small town in Ohio
Newly married
Both excitement and trepidation
Filled me with a sense of the

Momentous

The strange would become known
And, in time, familiar
And what would happen to me here
I knew, for sure, would alter

The relation of every star and
Far-flung galaxy
To every atom that had affixed itself
Into the center of my being…

As I pulled myself out of the
Safe cocoon of my trusted automobile
And closed the door
Sharply, with just the slightest

Hesitation

I took the first step on
This new parallel of latitude
Leaving behind the innocence of my
Nativity

While boldly embracing the mystery of
What was yet to be
Or not to be, for that
You see

Is always the question.

When First You See New York

And find yourself among
All those things you've read about
In books
All those things you've seen
In movies and television

Times Square
The Met
Central Park
The Museum of Natural History
Lincoln Center

Broadway

The Statue of Liberty
The Staten Island Ferry
Wall Street
Grand Central Station
The Brooklyn Bridge

Yankee Stadium
Greenwich Village
The Guggenheim
Carnegie Hall
Rockefeller Center

St. Patrick's
The U.N.
The Plaza Hotel
Macy's
Madison Square Garden

Suddenly
You are part of the myth
You are part of the dream
You have stepped into history
Get ready

To make your mark.

This One Place

The world is here
Here in this one place
We are in touch with all
That makes this human drama
So compelling

Music, art, theatre, history
Education, law, architecture
Finance, government
Industry

All is at its best
And all is at its worst

Here

The great outstretched arms of human
Achievement
Punctuate the skyline
Proudly proclaiming
The new birth of freedom

You can feel the elation of
Passionate lovers coupling in the
Neon night
Dreaming of an infinite
Possibility

Every blasphemous emotion
That anyone has ever felt
Struggles to
Survive and be
Recognized

Here

The suffering of so many tormented
Souls
Languishes
On every sidewalk and every
Back alley

People of every out of way place
Of every size and color
Speak a thousand different languages
Trying to find the common bond
That makes us all

One

You cannot walk these streets
Without confronting some
Heretofore unknown
Unexplored
Aspect of yourself

Look around you

Listen

Be aware

This is New York
Intoxicating and alluring

Offering itself up
To your most insightful
Introspection

Savor the experience

Feel what it is to be
Human

And alive.

Through the Back Door

Staying in an actor friend's
Apartment in
Washington Heights

Many floors up
With a great view
Of the bridge and the river

We begin our life together

Exiting the back door
Thrust like a quick jab into the
Stomach of Harlem

The noise and fume
Of incessant struggle
Chipped chunk of cracked cement

And shattered dream
Profusion
A litter of downtrodden

Humanity

Paper bags and rusty shopping carts
Lining the way to
Homelessness and despair

There is no escaping
The color of skin
It's in your face

Slapped like an unwanted
Badge of identity
Into your dim-witted

Consciousness

The things we have been taught
To distrust one another
To despise the different

Aspects of ourselves

We can escape down
The dark tunnel
Of a swift-moving train

We can pretend
We haven't seen things
That our eyes have

Shown us to be true

When we emerge
Up the stairs
And into the light of

Blazing blue sky day
The air is different
There is purpose and hope

From one mile to the next
From one block
To another

Everything changes

We have the power
We just don't have the
Will, do we?

To create, not to destroy
To heal, not to wound
To help, not to exploit

The back door
May be less visible, more remote
But we all know where it is

And who, at one time or
Another
Must exit or enter

For one man in his time
Plays many parts
And no part is a small one.

How You Hold Your Fork

I was raised in the Midwest to be a dolt.
I became one.
And it was good.
But one day, while driving
To the Howdiesburg County Fair
I got lost
And ended up in New York City.
At first, I felt like a duck in a china shop
But before long
They welcomed me with open wallets.
I was invited to the most prestigious cocktail parties.
They marveled at my wit:

> "May I bring you the humidor?"
> "No thanks, I already have a hat."

> "Have you seen the Van Gogh?"
> "No, I think it's still parked."

And when some jet-set hot-shot said,

> "I'll have my girl call your girl."

I thought he was trying to sell me a prostitute
So I called the police.

Yes, life outside the haystack has not been easy.
I've had a lot to overcome.
Like pork rinds and iceberg lettuce.
Why, I thought Roy Clark was hip.
That Elvis looked good on velvet.
It's taken me a long time to change my ways.

I no longer get my news from the checkout line
At Piggly Wiggly.
Now when I have steak, I don't serve it with Boone's Farm.
But still
There's one thing I'll always miss:
People who are what they are

And don't give a damn what anybody thinks.

Peeking Behind Door Number 2

Sluggo said to me
In his erudite way
"F--- you."
Then he punched my face
Through the wall
Old Joe, the bartender
Laughed
Gave the galoot another
Beer

Compliments of the house

Me, I rearranged my nose
Stuck my pennies
Back in my loafers
Limped across the street
To more comfortable
Confines
Hanging plants and steaming
Cappuccino
With just a hint of cinnamon.

The Algonquin Square Table

Before you start arguing about
This poem and that poem
Rhyme and meter, form or no form
Clichéd or original, good or bad
Influenced by this or that or
How could anyone write such
Brilliant unsatisfying
Drivel

Just let me remind you:
Poetry is not life.
Life is poetry.

An Actor Prepared

An actor experiences
Other people's lives
Through a metamorphosis of mind

Words sifted through a membrane of
Archetypal truth

Emotion held in space and time
And passed from body to body
Becoming real and imagined

On stages of humanity
Bound together
In the fabric draped from
Shoulder
    to
       loin

Footfalls on a distant planet
Three orbits from the sun.

Amadeus

wrote the most glorious music
with nary a scratch
heaven
      dripping
           through
the soft crack of his fingertips

a divine revelation
that only comes
through a gift of spirit

an ear in tune with the
silent
      space
that cradles the birth
of
stars.

The Broadhurst Theatre

The foot touches down
Plants itself on an old board
Not any old board
A board embedded in
Broadway history

The first step
No less than a child's
Brave abandoning
Having overcome the laws
Of gravity

I look around a sea of red
Velvet seats
Draped in balconies
Of admiration
Applause and celebration

They come to welcome me
The spirits of ages past
Decked in the tricks of their
Costumed trade
Made up, out of the imaginations

Of centuries of old bards
And two-bit players
Seemingly dead, but ever
Resurrected
For just one more

Commanding performance

They had their time here
Too:

Humphrey Bogart
Helen Hayes
Vincent Price
Rosalind Russell
Joel Grey
Ingrid Bergman
Colleen Dewhurst
Katharine Hepburn
Christopher Reeve

And many others will follow me
In the long procession
The seconds that spill from
Extraordinary clocks in days
To come:

Dustin Hoffman
Jason Alexander
Andrew Lloyd Webber
Jerry Seinfeld
Ian McKellen
Helen Mirren
Daniel Radcliffe
Al Pacino
Tom Hanks

You know them
If you pay attention
You feel their presence
You honor the experience
The gift that has been handed you
(Through no fault of your own)

And trusted to your keeping.

Mozart

had a voice

He had to sing
With the full force of his youth
Not caring what anyone else
Thought, like it or not
Cost him plenty, of course
In the political swirl of the
Age

He was after all
An artist

Ignored at the end
Rudely tossed out of the glittering court
Into the shallow confines of an unmarked
Grave

A shovelful of lyme to
Cover the stench of poverty.

Still Life

The masters all painted
Baskets of fruit
Why?
What is it about fruit
That demanded such passionate expression?
Was there a lucrative market of fruit lovers to exploit?

Personally
Fruit doesn't bake my cake if you know what I mean.
Now
Naked babes in the grass
That
I can understand
But apples on a dish?

What is it they're trying to say?
Do they tempt us like Eve?

"Buy the apple painting, Maude
Big, delicious, juicy, red apples
On a porcelain white dish!
Buy it, buy it, buy!"

Whisper the artist's serpent strokes.

Or maybe
'Twas some deep psychological need
That compelled the depiction of
Fruit.
There they sit
Inert
In a bowl, or basket or dish.
The artist as pear.

Brimming life
Immobile.
Contained within—

A precious seed
Waiting...

Why Can't You?

I can appreciate modern art
The play of form and line and color

I swoon to the classic stroke of the brush
The power in the finger of a Sistine God

I rock in the roll of rap and jazz
Thrill to the top of the high C tenor

I beat time with Mozart
Cry oceans with Dolly

O give me the hand of Martha Graham
And turn me on point with Balanchine

I revel in Shakespeare
And wallow in Ludlum

Eliot, Yeats, Byron and Shelley
We all share a toast and a smoke with Kerouac

Glorious creation, so easy to destroy
But the palette of possibility somehow

Prevails.

From the Top

The master
Rose slowly from his chair
Shifting his weight carefully
To the wobbling backbone of his
Cane

Straight enough to steady the onslaught of his nerve

A trace of spittle clinging to his beard
His eyes piercing the poof of each and every
Cod-pieced ego, poor players all
Heads in penitence
Lowered to the floor.

"What was that?!" he bellowed.
"This isn't soap opera for God's sake.
 Do it again and do it right.
 And remember
 Shakespeare is a blood sport!"

The Dancer

The faces peer from the corner of the room
And watch every move her willowy hands make
The fingers opening and closing
Plucking the strings of an untuned heart.

Her form glides without restriction
Parallel to the barre
Through the words that choke and sting
The careless musings of glass-eyed fondlers.

She will not bend to the indignity of an idle charm
Nor stoop in supplication of a whim
Her flight is measured in headlong leaps
An unyielding music that springs from her soul

A taunting pirouette on pointed toe.

Ghosts on Broadway

I remember seeing Anthony Quinn
Walking down the street
On Broadway in Times Square
And nobody paid him any attention
He was just another so-and-so
And who-the-hell-cares.

But I cared.

I liked Anthony Quinn
I recognized him
I knew the talents he possessed
In fact, my life was somehow better
In some small way, thanks to
Anthony Quinn.

That was worth noticing
On a crowded, self-interested sidewalk
Where people don't want to know who's
Walking in front of
Or behind them.

Washington Square Park in Fall

Washington Square Park
on a fall afternoon
cool breeze blowing
'neath a water blue sky.

Kids on a concrete hill
riding skateboard bikes
frolic on the jungle gym
laughing children's shrieks.

Young girl on a park bench
in a blue-jeaned sneakered pose
scribbles in a notebook
and dreams some faraway thought.

Black youth by the garbage can
rusty red bucket dented
mumbles to the passersby
disjointed joints for sale.

White youth tossing pigskin
in his stylish sports fatigues
tanned and bronzed like summer
muscles rippling on the green.

The middle-aged Joes play chess
black/white castles on the block
they send their dreams to battle
on ordered squares inert.

Old men sit in patience
cross their legs and heave a sigh
watching leaves go tumbling past them
like a memory

drifting...

Strawberry Fields

"Living is easy with eyes closed
Misunderstanding all you see..."

I remember when Yoko dedicated the memorial
To John
To all of us who imagined
That elusive, kind and peaceful world

Across from the Dakota where he was shot
Just off Central Park West at 72nd Street

I wasn't sure what I would see
But there were many
Many others who cared
Who brought flowers
Who wept tears
For what might have been
And what must be

We are the believers in a better world

We will keep the dream alive
Always
We cannot be silenced
We will not be ignored

Our eyes are open
Our minds are open
Our hearts are open

Peace, John
Thank you

We know that it's all right
As you yourself said

"Nothing is real
And nothing to get hung about
Strawberry Fields
Forever."

Lost Masterpiece

Michelangelo
Was born black in 20th century America.

He was a shoeshine boy and a waiter
A garbage man and a handyman

A store clerk and a construction worker.
In fact, he spent so much time surviving

He barely had time for his art.
He died when he was 50.

And no one ever heard of him again.

Lady in the Window

High up there
About halfway up the building
You can see her in the window
She sits there for hours
Searching the faces, the people in the street below
Wondering

Does anybody care?

Moving with purpose in their oblivious way
Making their appointments happily on time
Clocking the minutes of a prosperous day

Does anybody care?

In her sad eyes
She knows the secret
The terrible truth we hide in our lies
We are
All of us
Alone.

Does anybody care?

DIABLERIE

Inside walls, mirrors and
Sloping windows, sorcerers in suits
Midnight shades of black and gray
Ties twisted, stretching necks
Pretty assistants chained to clocks
Trap doors closed, ghouls in glasses
Pouring numbers in burning
Cauldrons, mixed and stirred
Siphoned into tiny vials for
Mass consumption
Boxed and labeled on
Conveyor belts to no-man's land
A poof of smoke in flash of
Pan
Abracadabra!

The meaning disappears.

East Side Ladies

The East Side Ladies
    are all very chic
fresh furs on their shoulders
diamonds in their ears
their shoes are never dirty
and their dresses always pressed
and they speak in clipped sentences
and sound like Cary Grant
    (with a higher pitch, of course)

One wonders why they hold their chins
    a little higher than their heads
and their eyelids but half-opened
    in a look of proud contempt
their chauffeurs rush to please them
limo doors snap open-shut
    then
they disappear behind the glass
and one can't see them anymore

But then one never could.

While Strolling Down Fifth Avenue

How much?!
Only $1500.
Oh, stop. It's gorgeous!
Isn't it though.
So soft. I've never seen a shawl like this.
Oh. It's rare. Very rare.
And sheer. Quite exotic.
Oh, but Prudence, you don't know the best part.
There's more?
Do you know what it's made of?
I have no idea.
Shahtoosh. Tibetan Antelope skin.
Nooooo.
And in a few years this antelope will be extinct.
You don't mean?
Uh huh. Think how much it'll be worth then.
Oh my God. Where can I buy one, quick?!

Watch Winding

I watch myself die each day
Winding 9-5
Clockwise
Meaning-less job
Making nonesuch for non-descripts
Dollars is as Dollars does
Check for the mortgage
Check for the car
Check to see that the check is paid
Check back to work to check it all again
Come home at last
Numb-brained
Collapse on the sofa
Turn the boob box on
Flickering and snickering foolish little man
Munch the junk
Body trash
Slow poison
This life
To bed. To sleep. Half-wake. Again.
Repeat. Repeat. Repeat.
Thumpa thumpa thumpa thump
Check the heart beat
Days to months to years and then
The dreams are dust
The soul is lost
How the hell did I get to hell
So soon
Before my time?

Just watch.

BRIDGING BROOKLYN

Brooklyn Bridge

sunrise on the bridge
light splashing through the arches
joggers chasing dreams

The Balloon

round and red
ubiquitous orb
chained to a string
and streamers silver
hanging suspended
  cl
     ing
         ing
     ten
   uously
  to
the tenement wire
stuck in indignity
on a broken stoop
lost and forsaken
unable to rise
helium ballasted
with weary time
no fluttering wind
to carry it home
its final gasp
here
tells of happier days
fanfare and circumstance
an open sky blue
and a child's loving hand
now bereft and

alone.

Field of Lost Dreams

Shortly after I was born
In Rochester, New York, in 1957
The Dodgers left Brooklyn

So when I moved to Brooklyn
Some twenty-five years later
Anxious to re-connect with the
Mythical figures of my youth
I felt that something was missing
The legend of those Boys of Summer
Had been lost and no one talked
About them anymore

Snider, Reese, Campanella, Hodges

They didn't even know their names
Dem Bums

And no one much remembered
Where they played – Ebbets Field

It took some doing, but I finally
Figured out where it was – the ball park
Or at least, where it used to be
And I hopped a couple of subways
To get there

When I finally found it
Something died inside me
It was just another ordinary place
So unimaginative, so unremarkable...

They tore the stadium down and put a big
Ugly apartment building on the spot
That reverent, irreverent spot

Ebbets Field — that held all those
Memories —
The emerald green diamond
That sparkled in the springtime,
Little kids and their dads laughing, cheering
Times that would never be duplicated
Ever again

Ballplayers who lived in the neighborhood
The Knothole Gang
The Sym-Phony
Hit Sign Win Suit

Gone.

History was made there
Important American history
But no one seems to care anymore
About history
Only a few old codgers like me
Who read books and dream of better
Days — when love meant more than
Making money

Only we, perhaps, still see in our aging
Mind's eye
Jackie Robinson taking that extra step off
Third base
Taunting the pitcher

Flying into the teeth of adversity and
Stealing home

Yes, whenever I think of Brooklyn
I think of the Dodgers
And I remember they left
Shortly after I was born.

Look Homeward, Angel

> "Where shall the weary rest? When shall the lonely of heart come home? What doors are open for the wanderer? And which of us shall find his father, know his face, and in what place, and in what time, and in what land?" –Thomas Wolfe, from *Of Time and the River*

It took a while to find
And if you didn't know where to look
You'd never know it was there.

The home I mean of Thomas Wolfe
— in the thirties —
The great Southern novelist.

I'd heard he lived in Brooklyn for a time
Same as me, rented an apartment, but where?
I finally found a
Reference in a book somewhere
With an address — the basement of number 40
Verandah Place.

It was my neighborhood, as it turns out
Just down the street
Somewhere below the Heights and the fabled
Brooklyn Bridge
But there was no marker, no monument
Nothing
To mark the history of this momentous place.

"Only the dead know Brooklyn," he wrote.

The building was owned by someone, so of course I
Couldn't go in, but I wondered if the owner even
Knew the significance of this brick and plaster and
Wood.

All I could do was look on from outside:
A tiny window at ground level, not more than a foot of
Exposed glass above the back alley black tar pavement
Dry leaves and dust stuck in the cracked and peeling
Paint of its frame.

The blind, pale and yellowing, was drawn
Leaving a cold and lifeless sense of a space
No longer occupied.

There was no seeing in, and it was a wonder to me
How that young visionary writer managed at all
To see out.

How dark, how damp this tiny room
Must have been, and yet
Here
Somehow was the birthing, light blasting
Through that little window
To catch the world's eye
A novel called, perhaps not without coincidence:

"Of Time and the River."

Brooklyn Rhapsody

11:30 p.m.
Of a Friday night
And the subway rattles out of view
Click. Click. Click.
His footsteps echo in the hollow station
The stench of urine
Cigarette butts, cups and clutter
Evident now by a bare watt bulb
Up the stairs
Click. Click. Click. Click.
And into the night
The darkness opens
Cool air and a sliver moon
Breathe once more.

No soul lingers
On the puddled streets
The futile crying of a recent rain
Street lights spackle still drizzling mist
Make sad monuments of the boarded warehouses
Tenement stoops
Baring their wounds
Graffiti slashed in mockery across the brick
Broken glass and a Coca Cola can
Kicked it clatters in the vacancy
Of night.

The leaves whisper
In the overhanging trees
Shuffled voices of a conspirator wind
The rolling dice rhapsody of a heartbreak
    Moon

Spills its secrets
Like a roulette wheel
And three dim figures appear
Non-chalant.

The first approaches
Innocuous line
"You got the time?"
(Step mid-road) "Sorry" (Keep steady)
The first persists
Circling behind
"Hey man! You got the time?"
(Shrug the shoulders, half a block, then home)
The second now in front
Head on. Straight.
"Yo! What time is it man!"
(Key in pocket, fingers ready, almost there)
The third is knifing at an angle
"Hey man! What time!"
Intercepting for the kill
Faster. Faster.
Behind, left and right
(Reach the corner. Quick)
"Hey, you! White boy!"
(Now. Break for it! Run!)
Three on one in hot pursuit
"Hey! Yo!"
(Grab the doorknob. Insert the key.)
"Yo, whitey!"
(Damn, won't fit. Faster)
"Get him. Get him."
(Faster. Won't fit. Won't fit.)

Fumbling hands
Running footsteps. Closer. Faster.
(Won't fit. Dammit. Faster. Dammit. Dammit. There!
Faster. Faster. Turn and—)
Slam.
"Ha Ha Ha Ha Ha Ha Ha Ha"
Hyenas barking to the thrill of the hunt
Blood lust. Burning. Three vanish
     once more
Their cackling litany receding in the night, silent night
Back to the door, the quarry gasping
Another night's respite, another night
Safe.

Something About the Hat

When she wore the hat
She became transformed
A woman to be reckoned with
No flighty, peroxide dish-head
To be emasculated by some un-masculine
Urge of a roaming bicep.

No.

Her nerve was grounded in the center of the earth
An unmatched beauty ushered from her form
A mystical power, borne across time
Channeled through the diadem of an Egyptian Queen
The wisdom of the ages gleaming
In her eyes.

The Winter of '83

Imagine a morning in February
Walking out of the subway
Onto an urban landscape
Of new-fallen snow
Almost two feet deep

No traffic
No people
No sound

This couldn't be New York City
Near Times Square?

Was I dead and gone to heaven?

Or was this some Twilight Zone
Serling forgot to mention?

The bright morning sun
Lighting up the wide white way
Of what I knew to be a street in
More troublesome times
Skyscrapers on either side
Traffic lights blinking aimlessly

The beauty of that surreal
Pristine moment
Lingers reassuringly
Absolute peace in a place
That had probably never seen it
Before

A real place, now
If only in a dream
A place I can return to
When all this confusion
Piles up in drifts of abstract
Human consciousness

Without making a shovelful of sense.

NAILED:
The Aftermath of a Bad Audition

the rope is tau(gh)t
inside my gut
nailed in-conviction
to the crumbling walls
of my battered heart
my head
shell-shocked

numb

a blunted spirit
the spark blown out
laid low in the depths of pity and remorse
i cannot move
let me leave the hurried world
and sink into sorrow
the dark, forbidden world

where no one can find me.

Prepared for the Worst

Rejection is so hard
For someone from Ohio
Where people smile and
Don't say anything.

Not like New York
Where rejection starts
Very early in life:

"Gootchie, gootchie, goo
 Baby say 'Dada' 'Dada'"

"F--- off, pops. I'm sleeping here."

It's Only Business

When he's not working
He's a perfectly likeable guy.
But put him behind a desk
And he becomes

Adolph Mussolini.

He'll stab you in the back
Rip out your heart
And toss you in the East River
All the while smiling

Assuring you that he is acting
In your best interests
And all you can say is

Glub, glub, glub.

Seafood Stew

Born into wealth and privilege
He thought the world was his oyster

Until the stock market dropped
And he lost all his clams.

Stage Kiss

The spot created a golden moon
On black-dropped canvas
Glittering tinfoil stars dispersed the light
The dashing hero in doublet and tights
His belly reined in a corset
Knelt slowly on the satin-looking plastic bedsheets
Leaned his tobacco lips
Down
To the waiting embrace
Of his cleverly-stuffed virgin-matron bride
Their mouths clamping together
For the obligatory five-count
Moving rhythmically for full dramatic effect.

The audience watched in rapture
Tears cascading down their cheeks.

As the curtain fell, the leading lady
Smiled endearingly at her handsome co-star
And whispered to her handmaiden
Through the clenched
Corner of her teeth:

"Remind me never to work with this
Pompous blowhard ever again."

Priceless Mementos

According to the courts

The objects had no value, monetary-wise:
An old broken watch his dad had worn in Nam
A pipe, a pair of nail clippers given as a
Christmas gift a happy smile long ago, and a
Torn, crumpled napkin signed by some
Baseball player, a Lou somebody, in a
Restaurant in the Bronx.

The Judge, glancing at her Rolex, eyes wincing
Scoffed at the effrontery of the youth
To presume that sentiment was of any
Consequence in the
Progress of a human life —

Gavel down. Case dismissed.
Heart broken.
Justice is done.

ADD AND SUBTRACT

Imagination plus Soul plus Discipline = ART

Imagination plus Soul minus Discipline = The Sixties

Imagination minus Soul minus Discipline = Chaos

Soul plus Discipline minus Imagination = Organized Religion

Imagination plus Discipline minus Soul = Science

Discipline minus Imagination minus Soul = Big Business

Soul minus Imagination minus Discipline = Death

The Woman in Black

Sleek, black comfortable skin
Glides across the stage
Barefoot, free

The white silk of her flowing robes
Catching the air mid-sentence
Holding her spine for an instant
Sublimely erect, then dropping
To the floor on bended knee
Arm to the breast, head bowed

With all the confident grace
Of one who has been there
Many times before.

The Comfort of Strangers

My neighbors surround me
Up, down, under and over
Apartment-style, big city splendor
In the brown weed, dying in cement
Faceless people, without names
Making noises in the night
Walls that cannot silence

The pain.

We pass in hallways
Stairways and landings
In and out of moving doors
Not noticing
The vacancy of moments
Never daring to ask
Or needing to answer
Preferring the dark distance
The shade drawn
With solemn fingers

To a comfortable close.

Saturday Night

In the crouch of a flea
A spot of grease upon the wall
The splat of old spaghetti

Arguments and insulted tears
Glued into the stems of drawn
Flowers perfectly lined on the paper way

The ear hears a hole
Someone's fist punching through
The solitude

Broken glass makes a beautiful
Kaleido scoped pattern
On the bare cement

Two stoops below.

New York Deli

It's a smorgasbord, I'm tellin' ya
Whatever you want, they got it
There's like so many different kinds of
People.

You thought I was gonna say Meats, didn't ya?
Well, I'm not much into meats, but I do like
People.

I mean people that are honest
People who tell you what they think
People who aren't afraid to be themselves
And these people aren't just any people
All of them the same
These people come from all over the world
And they speak a buncha different languages
You can't live in this city for very long
Without learning a hell of a lot
Of what life is all about.

That's what New York is.

It's the hope of the future
All of us working together
Getting along
And appreciating what each of us has to offer
To the Bigger Picture.

And in case you're wondering what the Bigger Picture is
I'll show ya
Just let me get my wallet out here a second
Yeah, here it is
See this.

You know who that is in this little tiny picture?
That's my grandkids.

And that's the Big Picture, my friend
That's the Big Picture.

Coney Island, 1985

On hot sunny sad summer days
When the vagrancy of my ambling life
Found no direction worth pursuing
I'd catch the F train
South, not north
A languid, lumbering ride

To Coney

Life's carnival there had seen much better
Happier days
The youth of a nation tarrying in such simple
Steeple-chasing amusements
The Wonder Wheel
The Parachute Jump

The Cyclone

A rickety roller-coaster ride
Hurtling along, exhilaration and danger
Careening along the rail
The ups and downs, relentless and punishing
Yet always finishing in a gentle
Gliding stop

But now the place was haunted
Concrete and steel crumbling
Fading billboards, chipping paint
Only the remnants of purblind memories
Staggering like punch-drunk boxers
To remain standing

The boardwalk, once thriving
Now deserted save for a few
Unlucky troubadours like me
Weather-beaten balladeers
Who cherish the camaraderie of the
Forgotten and forlorn

But after battling the vagaries of
The brutal confines of the city
This was a relief
To see the ocean
To feel the breeze

The smell of sand and sea is wild and pure

No matter how man might fail
To escape the miseries of the
Callous waning of his days
The Earth is always constant
Always true
The healing touch it offers

Always worth the sub-way's journey
To re-connect.

HOOK, LINE AND PIZZA

The pizza looked at me with
Pepperoni eyes and a
Green pepper moustache
Shoved his hot, cheesy smell
Into my face
Said, "Eat me before I
  Drip tomato sauce all over your
  Shirt!"

I had no choice, I was
Desperate.
I wolfed him down
With a quick swizzle of beer
And gave a resounding belch
  of satisfaction.

For a few brief moments
I thought that I had won.

But when I looked in the mirror
I knew that I had been double-cheesed
My crust stuffed to bursting
Another notch on the belt of that
Devious hombre's
Deliciously wicked ways.

The Dude in Leather Jacket

Put his arm around the tyke and said:
"Listen, kid
You want to pick up chicks you gotta
Do like I do:
Be a poet.
It's as easy as
2+2=4, word+word=sentence
You dig?
The chicks, they don't care what
You look like (good thing for me).
No, they want to know you can say things.
Make them laugh and cry and
Sure, a Mercedes and a credit card helps but
If you can sing in words
My friend
Play the strings inside your heart, well
I guarantee you
The chicks'll be flocking to your door.
A flock of chicks? Hmm, that's good.
I better write that down.
What?
What do you mean where's <u>my</u> chick?
OK. So maybe I don't have a chick right now, but
Let me tell you, kid
The truth is I spend so much time writing about chicks
And all the things they do that bug me, well
I haven't got time for a real chick. OK?!
Here. Here's a few bucks.
Go get yourself an ice cream cone or something."

Café Around the Corner

I take a mood-altering drug
To stimulate the alpha of my
Wave
Transport me to another level of
Apparent reality
My body swaying
In the saxophone breeze
Of a blue and white

Night

Yes, I do, I pop it through
The lips of my longing
Inject it in the blood of my vein
And smoke it in the cinders
Of my frequently fried brain
You can call it seedy
Or sleazy
Or whatever foul word you happen to like
Me, I just call it

Jazz.

Manly Man

Hey there,
Little man.

Name's Jack.
Big Jack they call me.

See that.
That's hair.

I've got hair on my chest.
You know what I can do?

I can flip a coin off my bicep
And catch it in my hair.

Women like that.

Chances

1 a.m. in Brooklyn
Out of the subway's cold, enveloping dark
The man emerges
Briefcase in hand, hurrying to get
Home
Wary eyes watching, glance in all directions.

The streets deserted, foreboding in the stillness
The light of lamps unable to spell the lingering dread
Shadows creeping across the brick
Inside vestibules where doors are locked.

Walking faster
Past shops barricaded with steel curtains
Fortification against the night
While somewhere in the deepening fog
A siren bleeds.

At the end of one long block
Another two to go
Just outside a closed café
Something on the sidewalk
By the sewer grate
Large and — what —?

A body.
Lies unmoving.
Alive or dead? What to do?
Finger nails polished, red on pale white skin
Female.
Face down, tucked and covered in dark hair.
What to do? To get involved in what?
In Brooklyn 1 a.m.

Not my business, not to know
He thought
Move on, she must be sleeping
Drugged or drunk
Someone else will stop.
The hour is late
A morning's rise at 6 a.m.
Meetings to be deadlined
No time to waste
She must be sleeping.
Someone else behind me
Someone else will
Stop.
Move on.

In the slanting rays of the rising sun
The bustling of a new and proper day
Keepers opening windows, shops
He walks past quickly
A bright café
An empty sidewalk
Nothing by the sewer grate
But stuck in his head forever
The nagging not knowing
Alive or dead? He didn't stop.

Subway Rider

The man was big, dark complected
Of some unknown nationality or another
Hanging on the pole, drilled to the floor
The olive green of his drab fatigues
Suggesting a military code (of mind perhaps)
The train trip-tracking down the line
Beating time
To the bump and grind of sad music
Humming 'neath the sundowned streets of the New York
City night.

The businessman sat across from me
Legs folded neatly at the knees
Short, trimmed hair and black-rimmed specs
Focused intently on the Wall Street
Journal
Numbers apparently whipping
Through his brain, a notch or two faster
Than the speed of sound.

Pulling into the station, nothing seemed
Amiss, the train jolting to its usual
Stop
But the big man – lurched – accidentally or
Not
His foot moving forward through
The businessman's paper
A violent, though brief burst of
Rage
That left the spectacles dangling
Shock on the clean-shaven face
Dignity decked without warning.

No one moved – stunned – not sure exactly
What
Had taken place in the New York blink of an eye
We watched – not comprehending – as
The big man calmly
Exited the train and
Made his way down the platform
The doors closing behind him with a
"Swoosh."

Brooklyn Nights

I'd like to know who I am
Inside your head
What crimes I have committed
In those back alleys of your mind
Distortions through the prism of eyes
    that turn away.

Maybe then I could understand why
Your hand withdraws
Your shoulders flinch
The cold sheets knifing
    through my back.

Moonlight through the window
Sprayed like graffiti
Seeps into the walls
Shadows of this life together
Incomprehensibly
    in code.

Words

Words have no meaning in the language of the heart

No sound
No syllable
No lettered thought

Can express the something
That dwells within the mirrored maze
Of human feeling

Only a touch
A look
A silent tear

Tells all
That can be told.

Kitten

I see two eyes
peering out at me from the corner of the couch
and a little pink nose
nestled in the middle
of bewhiskered, white marshmallow cheeks.

Uh oh.
What's this?

Two ears approach
(twice too large for that adorable face)
and gold and black eyes are wide
in mischievous anticipation.

Oh mortals, take heed,
such a slow methodical stalk
hath this monstrous, tigrous beastie.

See how he takes his position
on a twitching haunch
poised for the merciless kill.

Aha!

He springs
completely surprising my defenseless hand.

Little pink paw pads
are choking my index finger
but my defiant digit wrestles to the death!

Oh fearsome proposition
what horrible teeth you have grandma
those mighty molars strike terror to my heart
pray don't gum me to dea----Aaaaaaaggghhhhh!!!

(Damn cat.)

Two Timing

I took myself to a party
We sat in a corner
Nervous and out-of-place
With nobody to talk to but
Ourselves, and not wishing to seem
Unhinged, that didn't
Seem like a very good option

So we didn't say anything
We just looked at each other
And wished we were
Somewhere else, the other
So alone outside myself, I
Wondered how he could possibly
Keep it all together.

Famed

We were in the service of the man
Hired minimum wage
Casting a show
She and I, fellow actors, to read
Opposite other actors
Who were auditioning

He could do no wrong I thought
A blazing star in the theatre
Firmament
My idol since I was just a boy

But then

She came to me in tears
Some underling it seems
Had asked her—for HIM
Whether she would go out

"But I'm married."
She said.

*"Yes, but he wants to know
Will you go out?"*
The lackey replied with some
Embarrassment.

Funny, I didn't feel so bad
The next time that celebrated man
Looked through me
Without acknowledging my "Hello."

THE DAY JOHN MCENROE GLARED AT ME

I must admit, I wasn't a fan
But I got a free ticket, you know
To the U.S. Open in Flushing, Queens
Right near old Shea Stadium, Home of the Mets
And I *was* a Mets fan
Would have much preferred to see a baseball game
Than a tennis match, to be sure
Even if it was the U.S. Open

I arrived late, subways being what they were
Not always the fastest mode of transport
(and not the cleanest either!)
And as I entered the stadium
The match was already underway
Mock, mock, mock - the ball went back and forth
I had to find my seat
And it took a little time
People rising up to let me pass
I scooting dexterously in front of their
Sun-drenched, sporty shorts hobnobbing knees

I wasn't really all that noisy
But clothes do ruffle and feet do shuffle
So I guess it must have caused a gentle stir
As a deathly pall suddenly descended
Wrapped itself around me
An eerie discomfiture, like a sudden draft on a
Cold day in hell
And when I glanced at the court
Not far away, just a few rows down, in fact

There stood John McEnroe
Quite ready to serve
Ball in his hand, racket ready
But glaring at me, yes ME
The one who dared to MOVE
I was simply the most annoying little insect
He had ever had the irresistible urge
To swat, to death!

I sat down, finally, as I was, finally, able
Sheepishly, hiding behind my sunglasses
Hoping nobody would notice me
And realizing in a naive sort of way
That this was tennis, not baseball
A starched clean, cotton-trimmed
Rolex-wearing, orderly world
That I really had no desire to absorb or
Appreciate
Sorry, John, to have aroused your ire
A pity I didn't know any better

Someday, methinks perhaps, Mac
When you are lounging by your pool
Relaxing
You may chance upon a book of my poetry
That some studious worm had left
By maudlin chance on a nearby chaise
Like a free ticket to another world
You might take a glance, shrug your shoulders
Indifferently
And fling the flimsy thing carelessly away
Out of sight and out of mind

At that point, you might imagine, Mr. M.
That I am returning your vitriolic, eviscerating
Glare back to you, with my compliments
Then, in the proverbial way of "what goes around"
And only then, will you and I, Mad Hatters both
Be able to call ourselves "Even."

On the Road

Early in the morning, before rehearsals
A cup of coffee in the student union
Relaxing on sofas
Talking about anything and everything
Whatever came to mind, no need to
Censor random thoughts, subject
Out of taste or bounds
We were, in some odd way
Two different people, totally
In sync, engaged in the process

Of being

Human, without judgment or
Preconceived notion of right or
Wrong, somehow brought together
In this faraway place, defining ourselves
As we went, without limits
Open to the possibility
Of change in an instant
Believing that whatever happened
(Or happens) must be
Happening

For a reason.

Throwing Tomatoes

There are those who
Delight
In the belittling of others

Who take pleasure
In the nasty word
And the malevolent gesture

Some make their living
In the negative reaches of
Darkest space

They may call themselves
Experts or pundits or critics
But we artists know them simply as

Fools

Some things may deserve to be
Knocked down
But rarely are they human beings

It takes no genius to destroy

The creators, the givers
The lovers, the healers
These are the heroes who

Know

The building up
Is so much more difficult
Than the tearing down.

Man Called Thunder

Bold Warrior
Of the Setting Sun
Stands on the Rock of Imprisoned Time
The stony features of his darkened face
Ask no pity
Claim no piety
But iron eyes remember:
Burning lodges on a blood-red river
Broken arrow on Sacred Earth despoiled

A riderless pony gallops into blackness
And is seen no more

For screaming children
Slaughtered wives
The Eagle cries for Justice
And there is none
In a heartless land
But shallow men
Dig shallow graves
And in the gleaming of Long Awaited Moon
Lone Palomino returns from Midnight Pasture

And the Fallen Ride Again.

Hanging with the Devil

I hung out with the Devil on Manhattan's
Lower East Side

Had a toke of poverty
long, slow, heavenly inhale

The hobos burning dreams
'round a trash can full of fear

Anesthetizing homelessness
'neath a cold, dark scrapered sky

Pimps and whores were ticking business
like Wall Street whackers on the Stock Exchange

Longing Johns laid with riches seeded
in the backs of black-glassed shiny white limos

The tenements lurched in the chains of their indignity
shutters cracking in the wind

Babies crying, dogs barking
unheeded or unheard

And when I asked the Devil what tunes he'd like to hear
boom-boxing with the fumes of brake-dancing
    automobiles

He smiled in his ghoulish way
with a glint of fire in his eye and said

"Gospel."

The Second Coming

You won't believe me when I say this
Indeed I speak it still in fear
But the memory lingers with me, like the wound of a rusty nail
I saw the face of Jesus
Yes it's true
No please don't mock me
I did not believe it either, I did not recognize him at first
But then neither did the twelve in that dim ether long ago
His eyes were filled with love, inexplicable to me
And yet there was an anger and a sorrow, even fear
His hair was matted, rather dirty
And the clothes were worn and tattered, hardly elegant or refined
Yes, you laugh
And think I'm crazy
But I tell you that it's true
I saw the face of Jesus
Imploring and alone
If only I'd seen him sooner, but I didn't recognize him, you see
Till his body lay stiff and cold
Swaddled in the corner of the subway station, only ten or twelve years old
Homeless and forgotten
And believe me, you who will, with more venom than the Pharisees
Pontius Pilate and the rest
We have crucified Him

Again.

In Memory Of

His name is on a quilt.
It hangs in the museum.

People from all over
Come to look
At names they've never heard.

I just wish they could know
The person behind the name.

Then maybe they'd understand
The cost
Of what we've lost.

War in the Bedroom

Women are perfectly adept at processing emotion
In language, but men

Remain stuck in verbal catatonia
Unable to make common sense
Of uncharted territories

Not depicted
On maps.

Ringing

I meant it when I said it
I think there is no doubt
Yet there's a ringing in my head
I remember my hand was sweating
My finger yet unsheathed
Words went flying past me
But I uttered yes I did
Prompt-response and prompt-response
And words came back like an echo
From lips that I would kiss
I do. I will. I will. I do.
I Do Not Know
But somehow the lies were hidden in a guise of truth
A naive blinding
Mythic subterfuge
And idle vows easily broken
Senseless victims on a field of hollow dreams
Wounds and words are mixed in blood
Trickling memories
In and out
Of a two way mirror
Of holes.

Give me the words back
So I can spit them back in time
Where they belong.

Born and Died

You stood at the door, and left
without knocking

I awoke one morning
to find no one there

The cold space between you and me
unfillable

An empty box of eternity
wrapped in paper, on the doorstep

but no hands, capable
to open it.

Victims

there is sadness in her eyes now
an innocence lost
beaten by indignity and callous
misunderstanding
the arrows of life
wound with impunity
Cupid's bloody bow
is strung with a million hearts
wisdom bought at a terrible price
and love laid to rest
on the river of Time.

Curtain Down

the stage is dark
barren
my footsteps echo
hollowly
no one hears
but me
the swish of a broom
melodic
constant
the janitor bids goodnight.

i sit at the mirror
a face looks back
with tired eyes
hears the voices
that matched the faces
laughing voices silent now
faces detached
drifting
to their final resting place
in the twi-lit coffin of memory.

i step into the night
cold air
gently close the door
the lock clicks
quietly
like the latch on my brittle heart.

Gardens

A garden grows resplendent and fertile
In the hearts of a happy few

To have shared and loved, laughed and cried
The dew of our tears having touched the tender places

Where only the smallest petals
Have opened and closed

Basking in the sun of a verdant smile
Or hiding in the shadows of an overcast gloom

A garden grows
And sends its quiet roots into the singing soil of our souls

Breathe deep…
The rain falls but a moment

And in a moment
Gives life to another day.

Two Brothers

In a Greek diner in
The Village one day
Immersed in conversation with
One of my very best friends
As was our wont
On many a fortuitous afternoon
I realized, almost without realizing
My friend was what they call
A "black man"
An "African-American"

Hmm, I thought
What a curious thing
I hadn't noticed he was black
Not on this day anyway
I only recognized the truth:
He was my friend
It had nothing to do with skin color
Or any other human frailty of the
Imagination

There was no difference between
Him and me
We were brothers, that's all
Plain and simple

Sure, I had noticed his blackness
When we first met several years before
After all, that's what this society
Teaches us to do
To see the seeming difference
Between
One and The Other

I saw the dark enigma of his skin then
And I did as I was told
To be afraid of the unknown
To be afraid of the difference

That's what they tell us
To keep us all in line
To stop us from getting to know
One another
To keep us, perhaps, from coming together?

Why would they want to do that, anyway?
To keep us apart, to keep us in distrust
And fear?
Why would they want to stop us
From growing?

And who is "they," anyway?
Maybe it's we
Maybe it's us

What have we agreed to believe
In the fallacies of our illusions?

All I knew was
On this particular day
In this other-worldly
New York diner
There was no color in my mind
Or in my heart
I was truly free
We both were free

And as I shook his hand
Goodbye
His fingers warmly grasping mine
I felt damn good for all of us

All of us here
Amongst the living
And all who gave their lives before
On battlefields great and small
This was what it was all about
The real American dream
And it was worth it
It was a dream worth dying for
A dream worth living for
A dream that will eventually

Free us all.

Old Man and a Bench

Old man sitting on a bench
In the park
At the edge of town.
The paint is peeling
The boards rotting away
From years of pelting from the rain
But he calls it "friend"
This lifeless stone and weathered pine.
It gives him respite
At the close of day
Puts his weary limbs to rest
And brings a smile to his leathered face.
They sit together
The bench and he
Two lost companions
Fading in the darkness
Of the setting sun.

All the World

Shakespeare took poetry to the stage
And left her there
Singing songs
In the fire of footlight candles

The stars, in the open air overhead
Danced
To be immortalized in words
With Kings and Queens
Vagabonds and Fools
Stories to bard the ancient tongue

Now she bows to the curtain of another age
The taunts and jeers of a coarser crowd
The wisp of her hand still drawn upon the air
    in graciousness
Her gown retreating to the shadows of the wings

The stillness lingers in an empty house
When all have left, the play is done
But in the darkness, a presence
The corner by the window
The starlight peering in

Listening
A dream held in wait
Till she return.

LEAVING NEW YORK

Let Be

*"He would have proved most royal
  Had he been put on"*

But young Hamlet
Never reached the throne
Potentials lost in the dram of
Politics
His short life foiled
Treachery laced in a poisoned
Touch
A gaming room of doors
Without escape
We might well wonder
What could have been
But life, like an Old King
Plotting
Has its own ambitions
Often contrary, to the best
Fulfillment of our own.

Buffets and Rewards

The doors that slammed in my face
Like the walls that block passage in a
Garden's maze
Turned
   my head
      in new directions

One foot following another
An open space here

Another path's worn way
Beckoning there

Until I found a place perhaps
I, from the beginning, had been
Destined to know, all along.

Newton's Apple

I pulled out of the tight parking space of my divorce
Hit the gas and peeled out of Brooklyn
Forlorn hopes jumping off the fabled bridge
That everyone wants to sell, but only a fool would buy

But I paid no attention

Zooming past the broken dreams in the gutter walls of
    Broadway
Ghost mime gagging, tin cup in hand, choking on the
    breath of words
I sped along the Upper West Side where lovers once
    intertwined
In the hot central summer park night

The George Washington took me in its bow and shot me
    like an arrow
Into the hip of New Jersey, good for a laugh
To see the monstropolis shrinking in the dimming
    prospects of my
Rear view mirror

Farewell, New York
I gave you all I had of heart and soul, yet cannot claim to
    be responsible
For the mad break of humanity that sets us all on fire
Tragedy in the circumstance of our making

I ask for redemption in the exorcism of this great
Adventure

The road west, unexplored
Pulling toward some tantamount destiny

To shatter every notion of who I was
Or ever thought I'd be.

Vagabond Shoes

There's a tall building
On Central Park West
With a theatre near the top
And a balcony that looks out
On the wider world
Of New York City

I did a show there once
Early in my career
When the future I envisioned
Seemed as possible as it was
Alluring

And I'd hear Sinatra up there
Between the acts and the curtain calls
Standing on that balcony
Looking across the sea of rooftops
The green tree expanse of Central Park

*"Start spreading the news
I'm leaving today…"*
New York, New York
"If I can make it there…"

I was gonna make it, I knew it
It was only a matter of time
New York would be mine

Such are the fantasies of youth

And looking back
On the way that life
Actually transpires

The doors that never open
The will that is blunted by opposition

And the way each choice leads
To somewhere unpredictable
Trying as we may to steer our
Fortunes in a particular looked-for direction

I realize now, despite all the
Unfortunate setbacks, the dying of
Childhood dreams, the frustrations of
Not achieving one's formerly fondest hopes

Still, the journey has made a life
A life worth noting, a life worth living

Our stories make us who we are
And each story is its own purpose
And its own reward
Each story rings true and each story
Is worthy of the ages

There is no such thing as an
Insignificant life

Tell the story and be proud
To be counted among the countless
Generations giving birth to generations
Dreams giving birth to new realities

Humanity moving into the future
The universe ever expanding to
Infinity.

When Sinatra Died

The war truly ended.

All those men and women who gave their lives
The simple time of hero and villain
So easy to distinguish
Right and wrong, black and white
The myth of stripes and stars forever
Handsome Frank singing the virile baritone note
    of a confident generation
Swooning young ladies, skirts dipped below the knee
The red menace held at bay
By the will of moral authority.

Through the swamps of Korea
The jungles of Nam
Their sons and daughters caught in
Disbelief, seeking salvation
From unsanctified powers, out of control
The world trapped inside the twisted curtains
    of a nuclear age
Rhetoric corroding ideals
The skin burned in layers from the face
    of humanity.

But the wall came down after all
A measure of peace, a measure of sanity
The crooner laid to rest, laurels
Well-deserved in the hearts of a
Grateful nation
The wistful days of Big Bands and blue-eyed
Boys will always be remembered

The flag raised at Iwo Jima
Yet stands with honor
Half-mast in proud salute
To bid a fond farewell.

Cake in the Freezer

Today was the day
A day I remember

Too, too well
Almost twenty years ago
"The best day of my life"
At least, it was
Then
The dreams we had
Out of school, on our own
We couldn't see the road not traveled, yet
We believed
We didn't know, we couldn't.

I can't take it back
I can't give it away
I can't make it better
It just
Happened
A bittersweet memory that lingers
Beneath the skin
On certain days, like today

Much too close
To the surface.

A New Millennium

A Few Short Decades, More

The first twenty years, the sixties seventies
Passing by
Unformed and untried
Getting knocked up and down
Parents teachers school marm biddies
Trying to shape me into shadows of themselves.

In the eighties I was an actor
Trying to act my way through the curtains of
Myself
Without too much success, I might say
Tripped up by wires strapped
To the seat of my pants.

In the nineties I was a poet
Words taking over the loss of the past
The future looming with that inscrutable
Sneer? that mocks the best of
Intentions.

Now in the flip of a millennial dime
Still not sure and still not able
I cast my stone on a new adventure
Not knowing who will turn up
In the oncoming wave

This time

Only the change is certain.

Like Any Other

It was. A day.
He got up, grabbed a bite to eat
Kissed his wife and kids goodbye and
Hit the freeway.

Traffic was moving well for a change
Arriving to work 20 minutes early
Waiting for the elevator, then up, up, up
87 floors, dizzying heights at the top of
The World.

There was Bill in his rumpled shirt
Downing a cold cup of coffee and scratching his head
"How are you, Bill?"
"Just fine, thanks."
(Doesn't that guy ever go home?)

He sat down at his desk
Looked out the window, sun shining bright
The cars so tiny down below
The calendar said September
10 days wasted, he ripped the page on another day
11 stared back like a long lost dream
Not yet begun.

From his appointment book
A soiled scrap of paper
Found on the streets of Jersey
8 days after the fact, sad and horrible
Dawning on the sleeping dread of our
Realization,

His daughter's name "Susie" circled
In red, a big doodled smiley face and
A birthday cake—with candles.

What it must have been
As the plane crashed through the wall
The flames forcing him to the broken
Glass
No choice but one
His arms outstretched
Like an Eagle
Taking flight
Freedom in the fall of air...

O sweet God, to taste that one last breath
   of Freedom.

Tower 2, Floor 87

Someone told them not to evacuate
Smoke and fire gushing from the wounds of
Tower 1

...

It was an accident after all, wasn't it?
Not to worry, Mom.
I'm okay, Dad.

...

The phone, still attached to the wall
But the line so quickly dead
The world collapsing on itself

...

We let go of her forever
That last hope of innocence
Smothered in a ton of ash.

One September Morning

Suddenly

Life wasn't trivial anymore
People began to mean what they say
In dark subways, on dirty street corners
Strangers clasped hands
Day and night, black or white
The middle match of gray
Made safe in the blaze of truth:
The dollar dropping through the market
Numbers just ash, confetti to the wind
The smile at last come current with the sigh
The hug of a stranger more tender than gold.

Parents found their children in the rubble
And children afraid, were reassured
Death, always mysterious
Took his time and place at the table
The napkin folded neatly in his lap
But we, with hands enjoined
In prayer, this breath
Give our need to one another
The taste of bread and water enough
To keep this dream

Alive.

Where Have You Gone?

As a boy
I looked up and saw
Heroes on a baseball diamond.

Men making millions to catch and hit
A ball
How small.

They seem now dwarfed
By plainer men — and women
Those who work for a few dollars a day
Without recognition or praise
Those who risk their lives
To save a stranger
In the smoke and rubble
The ash of our collective humanity
Falling from the sky.

They didn't ask how.
They didn't ask why.
They simply did.

They believed in us without question.
And believing saved us.
Saved us all.

Differences

What is the difference between a black man and a white man?
Is there a difference between a Japanese and a Chinese?
A Bosnian and a Serb?
How about the difference between a Protestant and a Catholic?
A Muslim and a Jew?
Or a capitalist and a socialist?
Gay or straight?
What <u>is</u> the difference really?
A woman and a man, there must be a difference
Mustn't there be?
Oh, what's the difference <u>what</u> the difference is?!
The difference is
A beautiful thing.
Thank God for the difference.
Imagine a world without difference,
How would you feel about that?
Indifferent, of course.
So why don't we all just stop our moaning and
Complaining and go out there and

Make a difference.
It's a beautiful thing.

Return To New York

Return

Staten Island Ferry
Churning seaward cuts the harbor glass
Its crystalline wake
Diamond bright in the midday sun
Old man on the deck
Looks up at man-made mountains of
Lead and steel
They do not return his gaze
They can't of course
See
The wonder in those aging eyes
What dreams have we
That build our towers to the stars…

Ah there she is
Proud lady, standing tall
Her golden torch ablaze
Does she still care
These many years
A young lad then
Wept grateful tears
In the smoky days of '44
Never to return to the blood-stained soil of
His fathers' fathers
Orphaned
He surrenders his heart
To the maiden of the waves
Does she still care?

Follow the tear
In an old man's eye
And look to the beginning
Feel the hearts that beat
Unshackled joy
Forever to be
Free.

Good Old New York

You love it, you hate it
There's no escaping the
Mad impassioned voice of freedom
Crying from its streets
The hold it takes upon your heart

From the quiet oasis of Central Park
To the honking blast of Broadway
From the proud progressive stateliness of
Rockefeller Center to
The broken-bottle wasteland of
The Bowery

From the Cloisters quiet contemplation
To the swirling artistry of the Guggenheim
From the bohemian tree-lined
Greenwich Village lanes
To the posh pretentious shops of the
Upper East Side

From the cavernous vault of Wall Street
To the Empire State Building, the Chrysler
Madison Square Garden
Lincoln Center and the Met
And the ghostly place on the island's southwest corner
Where twin towers once stood like sentinels
Left a hole in the city's heart

Memories, dreams, and lost ambitions
New Yorkers will never forget

From Queens' ethnic neighborhoods
To Brooklyn's fabled bridge
To the House That Ruth Built
Buried in the hot, molten center of the Bronx
To the yearning howl of Harlem that
Refuses to be ignored

This is America
Like it or not
This is the place where Liberty stands
Boldly casting its light upon the world's
Darkest waters

No matter when you leave
You'll always come back
Its memory stings and suckles
The cold fresh slap of humanity
Full in the face
Honest and true

If there is to be a future
Spanned like so many bridges
Across the narrow straits of our divide
That future is

New York.

The Corporation

Grew and grew and grew
Generation after generation after
Generation
Swallowing company after company
Until one day it swallowed
The Whole World.

Ironically, having achieved its
Ambition
It realized it had to disguise itself
With a lot of smaller faces
To give the appearance
Of being disconnected—

So people would continue to
Believe
They were still independent
Unique individuals with
Minds of
Their own.

Soiree at the Met

Champagne in hand
Lips puckered in Brie
Thoughts dipped, like breadsticks
In the round
About way of old stale
Conversation

The businessman standing stiffly
His shirt stuffed
With the platitudes of
Gala openings past
Posits the age-old query

So what do you *do* for a living?

To which the poet
Tongue untied a little too loosely
Alternatively replies

I don't make much of a living
Sir
But I *do* live much of a making.

Warholed

I missed a decade
for the very first time

didn't keep up with
all the trends

fashions flying in one ear and
out my rear

oh my oh why I'm
out of touch

I don't know who
these people are

or why they aren't
important so

I guess I must be
growing

old?

The Players

Edwin Booth
The great 19th century Shakespearean actor
Founded the place
Across from Gramercy Park
In a beautiful Greek Revival townhouse
In 1888
Along with Twain
And William Tecumseh Sherman
Among others

Booth knew the power of
Great mind and heart
In a time when
Theatre, literature and learning
Were valued

How to bring together the most
Scintillating people of the age?

A gentleman's club
A thing of the past perhaps
With far too much machismo
But surviving in its antediluvian way
To this very day

Not just anyone can become a member
You have to be invited, nominated and seconded
And then you have to be able to afford
The dues

A friend of mine was nominated
And invited me along for the experience
A lovely lunch
In an immaculate portrait-laden
Wood-paneled room
Where, at only a few tables distance
I recognized a thin
Quite dapper, bald-headed fellow
Known to impertinent Americans as
Klink

Col. Klink of Hogan's Heroes, that is

His real name was Werner Klemperer, of course
(Son of the great conductor Otto Klemperer)
A cultured man, a learned man
An accomplished concert pianist, in fact
As well as a fine actor of considerable skill

And it struck me as odd that two different
Players, two Centuries, two different Americas
Were locked in cosmic collision here
The one, old venerable Booth
Known for his Hamlet
And the other, our modern-day Klemperer
Known for his Klink

The road less travelled?

I took the one marked "Hamlet"
If only I'd taken the one marked "Klink"
I might be one of The Players now
Instead of a poor poet who'll never be
Invited.

THE NEW NEW YORK

When the new replaces the old
Something will be lost
Is it something better?
Or something worse?
In the moving forward
Are we really moving backward?

The New York I knew
I loved
But when I returned
Many years later
After the fall of the Towers
That great day of reckoning
I no longer recognized
The familiar and the known.

The city was cleaner, even perhaps
Brighter
The slick facades
Gleaming with respectability
Colors comfortably complementing the drift
Of light and shadow
Sleek, modern, yet somehow
Reeking
With the stench of ruthless wealth and
Unbridled power.

Gone were the small oddities
The un-usual businesses
The locally-owned restaurants
Cafés, coffee shops, and diners
Each one a particular adventure
Into an immigrant's impossible dream

People you could get to know
Personally
And be glad for the acquaintance
So many different ethnicities and cultures
Coming together to find a way
To weave their stories together
Into a unified whole.

This was New York
The New York that I knew.

But now, I feel awkward
Puny
I am nothing here
And neither are you
The corporate monoliths
Loom high with their lording logos
The plastic, glass, and cheap perfume
Seducing and cajoling
Every last, loose dollar into a
Whirlpool of greed.

They look pretty enough to the casual
Eye – the buildings, the signs
The trim lines of each bustling thoroughfare
The men and women properly
Suited and ranked according to their functions
All of them young, all of them hopeful.

But where are the old ones?
The ones who have seen much
And know much
Much more

Where have they gone?
You used to see them everywhere
Battling for dignity in the merciless
Glare of this Big City brute.

And where are the poor
The destitute, the lonely?
Have they been removed
Like so much clutter
Swept from the floor and discarded
In the trash?

What are you now, New York?
And what will you be?
As we take a good look at our
American dream
We must ask the questions
Each of us, creating and destroying
As we go

Who are we now?
And who will we be?

Early Morning
Sept. 11, 2011

Ten years later
After the felling of the towers
I find myself in
Grant's Pass, Oregon

Many choices
Great and small
Brought me here
To this mountain top

A comfortable cabin
Away from it all
Away from the misery
That men create

As the light slips through
The cracks of
Night's forbidding
Shadows

Still lying in bed
Coffee in hand
Unwinding from
My slumber, I see

A family of deer
Appearing in the mist
As if in a dream
Just outside my window

I nudge my wife quietly
Beside me, she wakens
To admire
Three does, three bucks

And two little fawns...

It is hard to imagine
More beautiful, more graceful
More elegant creatures
Than these

They pause occasionally
As they feed on the dew-laden
Grass
To look at us

Looking at them

Slightly apprehensive perhaps
But realizing there was no
Threat
We were here to enjoy the

Peace of this morning
Together

If you ask me about
9/11

And all those who have
Died in bloody conflict

Since

I will remind you of the
Deer
Of the mountains, the trees
And the sweet green grass

I will remind you of
Other choices

And I will remind you of
Those fawns
Who look at you with
Innocent eyes

Wondering.

New York Minute

I.

In a New York minute
The world changed
Or so we were told

And somehow what had been
Before
Was now wiped away – forever

But what was left in the grounding of our
Selves
But rubble and ruin?

And yet—
There was a moment
One brief New York minute perhaps

When the world came together
As one heart beating in unison
With compassion for all

The loss, the grief
Had touched us all
And the way was made open for healing

We could have embraced each other then
We could have said let's build something
Better – together

We had the opportunity
We could have made a world for which
Our children would be grateful

But we didn't
We crouched inside our naked fear
Trembling in our unnatural loathing

Turning on the other, not seeing ourselves
In the cracked reflection of so many
Shattered window panes

While the voices of hate, the voices of madness
Cold and greedily calculating
Grew louder and louder

Someone made money, piles of money
Someone always makes money
When dreams are killed and people

Are crushed into nothingness
Of no matter and no
Concern.

II.

And where are we now
In this new (yet very old) barbarous world
Our consciences gagged and blindfolded

This lawless land
Of the obscenely rich and the desperately
Poor

Democracy slowly dying
The powerless many kept in their place
And justice but a byword whose true meaning

Has been lost like so many principles
From a pocket full of holes
Who

Is held accountable?
For these crimes against humanity?
These crimes against the Earth herself?

We have listened to the voices of hate
The voices of selfish unreason
For far too long

And yet we all know
Only the voices of peace will lead us
Where we need to be

Love doesn't make bullets
It doesn't drop bombs
Only hate does that – driven by fear

Who do we blame then?
No one but ourselves
We are the collective creator of our own

Agony.

III.

It is time for a re-awakening of consciousness
When we recognize the best in ourselves
And overcome the worst

I see New York again in my mind
I see it whole
People from all over the world

Living in this one place
Speaking in different languages, praying to different gods
Working together with genuine respect

Their children playing together as children should
I see them all, all are one
All are a part of the whole, a part of me

A part of you.

In a New York minute
I believe, we believe
We must believe

We will change it all over again
We will re-create and re-invent
Towers won't go down this time

Hearts and minds will rise up
Rise up and say: Enough!
We end these wars, we end this hate

We commit to each other's prosperity and well-being
We embrace all that is good
We heal all wounds and seek to end all suffering

Then at last we shall become
All that we were meant to be
From the very beginning

Humanity finally living up to its promise
Humanity finally becoming the fulfillment
And the salvation

Of its own improbable dream.

Photo Album

"Angels and ministers of grace defend us!" The role that convinced me to become an actor: Hamlet, Muskingum College, 1977, directed by Dr. Donald Hill.

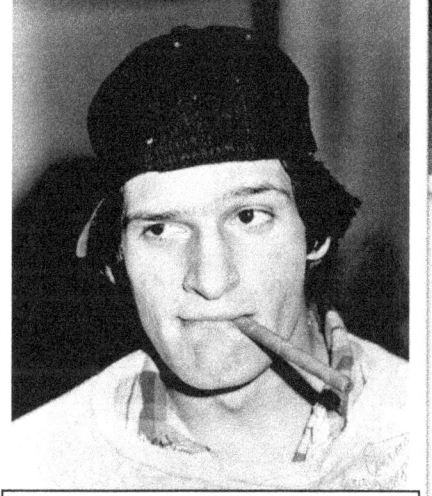

A comic turn as Oscar Madison in Neil Simon's *The Odd Couple*, Muskingum College, 1979.

As Oberon with Melanie V. Johnson as Titania in *A Midsummer Night's Dream*, directed by Robert Moulton, University of Minnesota, 1980.

On the roof of the Guthrie Theatre, Minneapolis, between scenes of *As You Like It*, 1982. That costume was one of my all-time favorites.

Here I am onstage at the Broadhurst just prior to curtain time for *Amadeus*, 1983.

West 44th Street, New York City. The Broadhurst Theatre (*Mary Stuart*) is sandwiched between the Shubert (*Blithe Spirit*) *right*, and the Majestic (*Phantom of the Opera*), *left*. I took this photo upon my return to New York in 2009.

To make ends meet, I took on several side jobs, including driving a horse and carriage almost identical to this one.

40 Verandah Place, Cobble Hill, Brooklyn.
The novelist Thomas Wolfe stayed in the basement in the 1930's with only that little tiny space at ground level for a window.
"All the underdogs in the world live here," he once said.

As Sir Richard Vernon in *Henry IV, part I*, directed by David Hammond, with Steven J. Gefroh (l.) and Edward Zang (r.), Yale Repertory Theatre, Lloyd Richards, artistic director, 1984.

Dueling Rock Stars. I played the upstart Crow vs. P.J. Benjamin's Hoss in Sam Shepard's *Tooth of Crime*, directed by Bill Woodman, Delaware Theatre Company, 1986.

As Sandy Tyrell with Patricia Fraser as Judith Bliss in Noel Coward's *Hay Fever*, directed by Robert Morgan, Studio Arena Theatre, 1987.

A chess board in Washington Square Park *(above)* just up the street from the Player's Theatre where I played Kanaka in Charles Busch's *Psycho Beach Party*, *(right)*, directed by Kenneth Elliott, 1988, photo by T.L. Boston.

As King Carlisle, with Dea Lawrence as Renne Vain in Charles Busch's *Vampire Lesbians of Sodom*, directed by Kenneth Elliott, 1989, photo by T.L. Boston.

As Jed Jenkins with Jack L. Davis as Kenneth Talley Jr. in *Fifth of July*, directed by Andrew Glant-Linden, Equity Library Theatre, 1989.

As Jonathan Harker *(above)* in *Dracula* with Sarah McCord Williams as Mina Seward, directed by Robert Spencer, Meadow Brook Theatre, 1990.

As Bob Cratchit *(right)* in *A Christmas Carol* with Wil Love as Scrooge, directed by Carl Schurr, Totem Pole Playhouse, 1990.

With a new headshot, I was ready to leave New York and embark on a new adventure in Hollywood, 1991, photo by Joe Abaldo.

St. Paul's Chapel, Trinity Church *(above)*, located near the intersection of Broadway and Wall Street, became a refuge for people escaping the debris cloud on 9/11.

Upon our return to New York in 2009, we were moved to find memorials like this one inside St. Paul's, helping us all to heal *(below)*.

Broadway and Wall Street, art and commerce – "strange bedfellows" as Shakespeare might say.

After visiting my old neighborhood in Brooklyn, my wife Nancy and I just had to walk across the Brooklyn Bridge!
(Photo courtesy of the kindness of strangers.)

LINER NOTES

LINER NOTES

Whenever I read a poem, I wonder what the impetus was that compelled the poet to write the poem. Moreover, I find myself wanting to know more about the poet. What is the life experience that gave birth to the perspective? It is, after all, a rare breed of human being that devotes him- or herself to poetry, especially when the art form is so misunderstood, mocked, and even vilified by so many in our modern American culture.

To me, poetry is music. I grew up in the age of Rock and Roll and record albums. Many of my favorite poets were musicians like Lennon and McCartney, Bob Dylan, John Denver, Paul Simon, Neil Diamond, Joni Mitchell, Joan Baez, Leonard Cohen, Bruce Springsteen, Judy Collins, Billy Joel and so many more. These liner notes are provided, as on a record album, for those adventurous few who want to know more, who want to dig beneath the surface and discover a little bit about the back-story that produced the poems.

Crossing the Hudson (p.3). Moving to New York in the spring of 1982 was a huge risk. There were no jobs waiting for us. My wife and I would have to start from scratch and make a go of it somehow. We had a little money in the bank, but not much. The feelings we experienced, full of hope, anticipation and trepidation, were not unlike any immigrant who has to leave the known world behind and come to a totally unknown New World of unforeseen challenges.

Through the Back Door (p.10). We first rented a place in Washington Heights overlooking the George Washington Bridge and the Hudson River. It was beautiful. As soon as we walked out the back door – literally – we were in Harlem. We took the subway from Harlem to get to the main parts of Manhattan, particularly the Broadway district and the Village, where I initially spent much of my time looking for acting work. The extreme juxtaposition of Harlem and Midtown Manhattan had an unnerving impact. I was confronted with the issue of color, of opportunity (or the lack thereof), and of social class. New York is like that, changing drastically from one neighborhood to the next.

How You Hold Your Fork (p.13). I thought I was pretty well educated when I went to New York, but I soon learned how innocent and naive I truly was. A director actually joked to me after an audition, "I'll have my girl call your girl." Believe it or not, that was an expression I had never heard before. This poem came out of my embarrassment. New Yorkers, like Midwesterners, by the way, are very comfortable with who they are. They don't give a damn what anybody thinks either.

The Algonquin Square Table (p.16). I've always been an admirer of the creative camaraderie of those artists and intellectuals who were part of the Algonquin Round Table: Dorothy Parker, Robert Benchley, Harpo Marx, Alexander Woolcott, Heywood Broun, George S. Kaufman and others. I've often yearned to become part of such a group, but regrettably, I have never found anything like it in all my years of creative endeavor. The poem is perhaps a leap into an imaginary roast of my own work. What would the critics, the erudite wits have to say about my poetry? And would I care?

An Actor Prepared (p.17) is an allusion to the famous work by Constantin Stanislavski, *An Actor Prepares*, the book I studied closely as I was beginning to learn my craft as a student at Muskingum College in Ohio. I was very proud to be a professional actor and still am. To be an acrobat of the heart, mind and soul is a prodigious artistic achievement that deserves the utmost respect.

Amadeus (p.18) means "love of God." Having been cast in *Amadeus* on Broadway in the late summer of 1982, my life became totally immersed in the life experience of Wolfgang Amadeus Mozart. Every night on stage, I reveled in the glorious music of this masterful genius. Life was made beautiful by art. Even when I went home, I chose to listen to classical composers instead of rock musicians for the first time in my life.

The Broadhurst Theatre (p.19), located at 235 W. 44th St. in Manhattan, opened in 1917 and has played host to many notable productions including *The Petrified Forest* (1935), *Auntie Mame* (1956), *Oh, What a Lovely War!* (1964), *Cabaret* (1966), *The Sunshine Boys* (1972), Bob Fosse's *Dancin'* (1978), *Death of a Salesman* (1984), *Broadway Bound* (1986), *Les Miserables* (2006-2008), *Equus* (2008), *The Merchant of Venice* (2010) and *The Front Page* (2016). My dressing room was on one of the upper floors of this venerable theatre. Before the show, I would crawl out the window to the fire escape and gaze down at the activity on 44th Street below and across the street to the St. James Theatre (where the Academy Award winning film, *Birdman,* was shot in 2013). When I was not onstage, I often retreated to my dressing room to work on a play I was writing called *Slingshot,* my first serious and disciplined attempt at writing. The nightly exposure to the genius of Mozart was inspiring me to pursue my own creative gifts. Not only that, my fellow dressing room mate, actor Ben Donenberg, was also inspired to write a script, a comedy spoof called *Starship Shakespeare.* The

165

two of us could be found between scenes furiously scribbling away on our respective works. Ben's play eventually led to his becoming founder and executive artistic director of the Shakespeare Center of Los Angeles (SCLA).

Mozart (p.21). The life of an artist is not easy. Mozart's tragic end is not unlike many others who dedicate their lives to their art. There is always an element of risk, daring and sacrifice to any great creative achievement. Many worthy artists never make much money or achieve fame. Of course, money and fame are not what most artists are all about.

Still Life (p.22) was written on Aug. 30, 1986. I used to frequent the Met and the Museum of Modern Art. This poem was inspired by the experience, I suppose, and I began to realize that the still life could be a metaphor for so many artists who are trying to emerge and make their mark.

Why Can't You? (p.24). There is so much misunderstanding about art in this country. Most Americans have little art education and certainly no appreciation of art in all its various forms. Art ennobles and enlightens. It makes our lives more beautiful and more meaningful. Too many have never experienced it or have any idea what they're missing. In 1987, I began working as a teaching artist for Lincoln Center Institute in order to share my love of all the arts with others. That passion continues to the present day.

From the Top (p.25). This one was inspired by a real-life story told to me by my wife Nancy McDonald about a teacher she had when studying in London. Shakespeare and soap opera are diametrically opposed. The first is literate, poetic and philosophical; the second is commercial. I worked on many soap operas while in New York, at first doing small roles and eventually playing featured guest roles including Rev. Kevin Burns on *All My Children*, who married Nico and Cecily, and a psychopathic killer named Oliver on *Loving* who was finally gunned down in a dramatic fight scene. As an actor and artist, I much prefer the theatre to film and television. The work itself, both in rehearsal and in performance, is so much more interesting and fun, at least for me. Nothing can surpass the thrill of a live theatre audience while creating the arc of a character from start to finish. Plus, you really get to know your fellow actors working together day after day and night after night. In TV and film, most of your time is spent sitting around waiting, then shooting scenes in piecemeal – take after take after take. It can be exhausting and tedious. Of course, comparatively speaking, you never get paid much to work on the stage, nor will you achieve the fame, the glamour and the glory that the film and TV world bestows.

Washington Square Park in Fall (p.28). This is one of my earlier poems. I sat down on a bench on Oct. 5, 1987, in Washington Square Park in Greenwich Village, looked around me and wrote this poem. The green spaces of the city are like so many oases, so necessary to help us all maintain our physical and mental health.

Lost Masterpiece (p.32). There are so many artists of all colors who have to sacrifice their art in order to make a living. It's a tragedy. The most creative people (and often the most compassionate) are not supported in our culture. It is a constant struggle to survive.

Brooklyn Bridge (p.41). Of all the things to do in New York, my favorite was to walk across the Brooklyn Bridge, typically starting from the beautiful and historic Brooklyn Heights neighborhood, then crossing into Manhattan and back again. If you haven't done it, you really should. It doesn't cost a dime and the memories last a lifetime.

The Balloon (p.42). I wrote this one on May 22, 1989, inspired by the quiet streets and brownstone row houses of residential Brooklyn. Every object has a history, doesn't it? There are ghosts everywhere, stories long past that never get told. If we listen closely, we might hear them, but in the end, all we can do is wonder.

Brooklyn Rhapsody (p.48). This is a true story. A real life experience – and a terrifying one. It took place one night while coming home after an evening's performance of *Amadeus*. Every night after work I had to walk through a dark and deserted neighborhood from the subway station to my apartment building located across from some projects in Boerum Hill, Brooklyn. The possibility of getting mugged was ever present. Those who have never lived life on the edge have no real understanding of what it means to be poor.

Nailed: The Aftermath of a Bad Audition (p.54). This was one of my earliest poems jotted down shortly after a particularly awful audition I did for the Walnut Street Theatre in Philadelphia. Putting my feelings into words was cathartic. Eventually, I learned not to give auditions so much emotional weight, to chalk each one up to experience. Rejection for an actor is constant and continuous. It can really batter your ego and self-esteem if you let it.

It's Only Business (p.56). As a poet seeking truth, of course, I have never been adept at being a cutthroat businessman, nor would I ever want to be. I grew up thinking life was about being kind and helping people, but hey, that's just me.

Priceless Mementos (p.59). This poem came out of a legal dispute as a young man took his case to small claims court. The items he lost meant an awful lot to him, but not to the court. For me it brought up the whole idea of values. What are the things we value as a society? How have those values changed over time? Do we value the things that are invisible like love and honor and caring and giving? A crummy napkin with Lou Gehrig's signature might not have any monetary value in a court of law, but it certainly has value to anyone who knows anything about Mr. Gehrig and the worthy example he set for us all as a human being.

Hook, Line and Pizza (p.68). Pizza has always been my favorite food. I loved New York pizza that you could fold in your hand and eat on the run. Later, when I learned about animal cruelty on factory farms and the damage that animal agriculture was doing to the environment, I gave up the pepperoni, the sausage and the cheese for the sake of the Earth and my own conscience. Happily, my heart became a heckuva lot healthier as a result. My high blood pressure and high cholesterol numbers dropped dramatically to normal levels. Today, I make a mean no meat no cheese pizza that is absolutely de-lish!

Subway Rider (p.74). Another true story. I was a witness to the event. Animosity is hiding just below the surface of our everyday lives and may strike at the most unexpected of times. The phenomenon will only intensify as our estrangement from one another becomes more pronounced in our politics and our culture.

Words (p.77). This poem came into being on Apr. 12, 1986. Our ability to express ourselves in words somehow always falls short when it comes to the greatest truths of life and relationship. Poetry is the art of using language to transcend language. Prose pretends to be straightforward in its application to the truth, but truth itself is a dissembler. Poetry, much more honest, knows the deception can't be overcome. We writers do our best to find a place of resonance, to illuminate some deeper meaning within the mystery.

Kitten (p.78) was written on May 14, 1986. Some friends of ours gave us a kitten as a gift. Not long before, I had returned to Brooklyn after performing *Twelfth Night* at Alaska Repertory Theatre in Anchorage. I named the little guy Kenai after a peninsula in that great state. He brightened up my life in so many ways. I still miss him dearly.

Famed (p.81). Fame brings power. Power, sadly, corrupts the heart and soul. The famous may begin to believe in their own celebrity. It's all an illusion, of course, but they lose touch with what it means to be powerless, to struggle in a world without opportunity. Women, unfortunately, are often slighted and abused by powerful men. It's wrong, of course. Everyone should be treated with kindness and respect. Always.

The Day John McEnroe Glared at Me (p.82). This poem is a little tongue-in-cheek, though it really did happen. In fact, I enjoy John McEnroe's bad-boy persona and completely understand his devotion to, and intense focus on, his game.

On the Road (p.85). Occasionally in life, you meet people with whom you hit it off instantly. That was the case here when I was performing *Dracula* at the Meadow Brook Theatre located on the campus of Oakland University in Rochester, Michigan. Strange as it may seem, I had few acting opportunities to work in New York City itself. Auditions for Broadway or Off-Broadway shows were rare. Consequently, I often went "on the road" to work. Every time was a new adventure that brought a sense of freedom and relief from the continual ongoing struggle to look for my next acting job. I saw parts of the country I would never have seen otherwise and developed friendships that have lasted to this day.

Man Called Thunder (p.87). We sometimes forget that the Native American story is always with us, even in New York. Written in December of 1985, this was one of my earliest poems inspired as it was by an experience I had while working as an actor for the Simon and Kumin Casting office. One day, we auditioned an elderly Native American actor named Rino Thunder for a play about Native and Mexican Americans. As he read the script aloud filled with vulgar, expletive-laden language, he suddenly threw it down on the floor and exclaimed, "This is not who we are!" He got up and walked out, refusing to be a part of it. He made a profound impression upon me, standing as he did for human dignity and the honor of his people. I recently found out that he eventually fell on hard times, lived as a homeless man in Tompkins Square Park and died in 2003 at the age of 69. According to his obituary in *The Villager* (Vol. 73, No. 22, Oct. 1-7, 2003), he was very much loved and respected for his wisdom, kindness and concern for others. I honor his memory here with the publication of this poem.

In Memory Of (p.90). The AIDS Memorial Quilt was established in 1987. As I was growing up in the sixties, America was a fairly homophobic and racist place. I had a lot of learning to do in my evolution as a more compassionate human being. Many of my theatre friends were gay and, as fate would have it, I was cast in several LGBT themed works including not only Lanford Wilson's *Fifth of July*, but also Charles Busch's comedy hits *Vampire Lesbians of Sodom* at the historic Provincetown Playhouse and *Psycho Beach Party* at the Players Theatre in Greenwich Village. I even played a gay man coming to terms with his gender-related psychological issues on the *Dr. Ruth Westheimer Show*. Several of my friends and colleagues tragically died of AIDS in the eighties and nineties. I loved them all for who they were. Their plight compelled me to become a civil rights and gay rights activist, to do my part to fight against prejudice, persecution and injustice.

Curtain Down (p.95) was written on July 17, 1986, as I was flying on a plane to Colorado to visit my aunt and uncle. I had just closed *The Red Rose* for Lincoln Center, a retelling of the fairy tale, *Beauty and the Beast*. Every show has a sad ending when it closes, when you have to part from those whom you have gotten to know and love. In the back of your mind you know that you will probably never see them again. Life is like that, too.

Gardens (p.96) was written upon the closing of another show of mine on Feb. 26, 1989: Lanford Wilson's *Fifth of July* for Equity Library Theatre in New York City. This poem takes a much more positive and comprehensive look at the endings in our lives – all of our experiences make us who we are. If we can appreciate each experience and look forward to the possibilities opening before us, we will live our lives with a certain kind of grace and meet our own ending with peace.

Let Be (p.105). I played Hamlet when I was a sophomore at Muskingum College. That experience convinced me that I had enough talent and passion to become a professional actor. From then on, Shakespeare's words inhabited my mind. After all, I had memorized much of the entire play. Later, I would play Romeo in *Romeo and Juliet at* Muskingum; Oberon in *A Midsummer Night's Dream* at the University of Minnesota; Adrian and Ariel (understudy) in *The Tempest* and a Lord to Duke Senior in *As You Like it* at the Guthrie; Sir Richard Vernon in *Henry IV, part 1* at Yale Repertory; Curio in *Twelfth Night* at Alaska Repertory; The Duke of Aumerle in *Richard II* for Riverside Shakespeare Company; Laertes in *Hamlet* at the Nashville Institute of the Arts; and Antipholus of Ephesus in *Comedy of Errors* at Meadow Brook Theatre in Michigan. My fondest hope as an actor, in fact, was to work as much as possible in Shakespearean plays. I would have liked to perform the entire canon. Unfortunately, there just weren't enough opportunities to realize that dream. So many dreams are killed by lack of opportunity, aren't they? Nevertheless, I was able to channel my love of Shakespeare into my own verse. You may find the Bard's words, phrases and literary techniques cropping up here and there throughout my work. I give him full credit for being a guiding light.

Vagabond Shoes (p.109). The show in question was *Summit Conference* by Robert David MacDonald for New York Studio Theatre. It was performed at TOMI Theatre, 23 W. 73rd St. I had a glorious rooftop view that I would soak in as the sun was setting before many a pleasant evening's performance.

When Sinatra Died (p.111). My older brother David was a huge Sinatra fan, so I heard Ol' Blue Eyes all the time as I was growing up. His death on May 14, 1998, was heartbreaking for a lot of people who loved him.

A Few Short Decades, More (p.117). With the coming of the new millennium, I reflected on where I was and where I had been, never knowing, as always, what the future had in store. I was living in Columbus, Ohio. I had had some success in publishing my poetry in various journals and magazines and I had awakened a passion for genealogy, for discovering my ancestral roots.

Tower 2, Floor 87 (p.120). On January 17, 2000, I was lucky enough to marry my soul mate, Nancy McDonald. We led parallel lives as it turned out. She was an actress in New York all the time that I was there. We didn't meet, however, until we had both moved to Hollywood in the early 1990's. We were living in Oregon when 9/11 happened. This poem was written in honor of a woman Nancy knew in New York, who perished on that terrible day.

Return (p.127). This poem was inspired by a man I saw while riding on the ferry from lower Manhattan to Staten Island. Poetry itself is, in many ways, a return to a familiar place, a re-visitation of a memory. Hanging on to the best parts of ourselves and moving forward with our dignity intact is one of the great challenges of our lives, both personally and as a nation. Will Lady Liberty continue to be a beacon of light? Or will we succumb to the worst in ourselves and turn our backs on the rest of the world?

The Corporation (p.131). In the thirty-five-year span of my relationship to New York, I have witnessed the takeover and makeover of the city by corporations. Corporations aren't people, as some unscrupulous greed-merchants would have us believe. That's absurd. They exist to make money – huge amounts of money. They have no conscience and no heart. If we allow a ruthless corporate culture to dominate our lives and our world, the future for humanity will be very bleak indeed.

Soiree at the Met (p.132). As an artist, I have made very deliberate choices in my life to uphold my personal integrity and fulfill my creative gifts. I have never been seduced by the lure of money and power. It doesn't interest me. Materially-speaking, I have very little and I like it that way. I am close to the Earth. But do not be deceived; I am a very rich man. I live a life of continual wonder in a world of love and beauty, no matter what is going on in the wider world around me. New York educated me, awakened me, and helped me to discover the best parts of myself. For that, I am forever grateful and indebted to the city, its vibrant spirit and all its inhabitants. I was changed in a New York minute and you will be, too, if you give it the chance.

ACKNOWLEDGEMENTS

Grateful acknowledgement is made to the editors and publishers of the following periodicals and web journals in which poems in this collection first appeared, some in slightly different versions.

Aabye's Baby, "Famed"

American Muse, "All the World"

Angelflesh, "Ringing"

Art Villa, "Still Life"

Ascent Magazine, "Lady in the Window"

Bardo Burner, "Old Man and a Bench"

Bulk Head, "Peeking Behind Door Number 2"

The Centrifugal Eye, "Brooklyn Nights" "Saturday Night"

Comrades, "On the Road"

Emotions, "Victims"

Footprints, "In Memory Of" "Return"

The Hold, "Café Around the Corner"

The Inditer, "Lost Masterpiece"

Ixion, "Washington Square Park in Fall"

Kookamonga Square, "Chances"

MiPo Magazine, "Hanging with the Devil"

Nuvein, "Watch Winding"

Office Number One, "Manly Man"

Poems Md, "Brooklyn Bridge"

Poetry.com: "Tower 2, Floor 87"

Poetry Soul to Soul: "Gardens" "The Second Coming"

Poets International, "Diablerie"

Short North Gazette, "Kitten" "War in the Bedroom"

Some Words: A Place for Poetry, "East Side Ladies"

Stroll of Poets Society, "Differences" "Words"

EWG Presents: This Hard Wind, "Man Called Thunder" "One September Morning"

Wings, "Curtain Down"

Wired Art from Wired Hearts, "Brooklyn Rhapsody"

The following poems were published by Indelible Mark Publishing in Mr. Overmire's previous books:

Gone Hollywood, "An Actor Prepared"

Honor and Remembrance, "Like Any Other"

AUTHOR BIOGRAPHY

Laurence Overmire has had a multi-faceted career as poet, actor, director, educator, genealogist and public speaker. He is the author of 11 books. He first began to seriously consider an acting career while a student at Muskingum College (now University) in New Concord, Ohio, where he starred in many productions including the title roles in *Hamlet* and *Romeo and Juliet*, El Gallo in *The Fantasticks*, Oscar in *The Odd Couple* and Tom Wingfield in *The Glass Menagerie*. Upon graduation in 1979, he was awarded a Bush Fellowship to attend the University of Minnesota where he played Oberon in *A Midsummer Night's Dream* and Dr. Carrasco in *Man of La Mancha* while completing his M.F.A. in acting. He won a second Bush Fellowship to become a professional actor with the renowned Guthrie Theater in Minneapolis during the 1981-1982 season under the artistic directorship of Liviu Ciulei. It was a season that featured Hume Cronyn and Jessica Tandy performing the American premiere of *Foxfire*. Overmire appeared that season in *The Tempest* directed by Ciulei and starring Ken Ruta, Boyd Gaines and Frances Conroy; the American premiere of Nelly Sachs' *Eli: A Mystery Play of the Sufferings of Israel* directed by Garland Wright; *As You Like It* starring Val Kilmer and Patti LuPone; and a classic staging of *Our Town* directed by Alan Schneider. The Guthrie's annual production of *A Christmas Carol* was filmed that same year for television with Overmire playing Albert Hall and several other parts.

At the end of his Guthrie stint, Overmire got married and moved to New York City, quickly landing acting jobs in *Don Juan*, directed by Richard Foreman for Joseph Papp's New York Shakespeare Festival in Central Park and *Amadeus* at the Broadhurst Theatre on Broadway directed by Sir Peter Hall and starring Frank Langella and Mark Hamill.

Off Broadway, he became part of Charles Busch's acting company performing in the comedy hits *Vampire Lesbians of Sodom* and *Psycho Beach Party*. He also played The Beast opposite Tracy Kolis in Lincoln Center Institute's version of *Beauty and the Beast* (titled *The Red Rose*) and Jed Jenkins in Equity Library Theatre's revival of Lanford Wilson's *Fifth of July*. Overmire travelled extensively around the country performing in various regional theatres: Yale Repertory, Alaska Repertory, Delaware Theatre Company, Nashville Institute of the Arts, Studio Arena Theatre, Meadow Brook Theatre and Totem Pole Playhouse. He had numerous roles on many television soap operas including *All My Children, One Life to Live, Another World, As the World Turns* and *Loving*.

Following a divorce, Overmire packed his bags and embarked on a whole new career adventure on the West Coast in 1991. There he met the love of his life, actress Nancy McDonald. In Hollywood, he became executive producer of The Writer's Lab to develop quality scripts for film and television, working with many fine actors and directors including Lucy Liu, Ted Lange, Debra Jo Rupp, Hill Harper, Mike Evans, Richard Schiff, Kevin Meaney, Jerry Lambert, Robin Curtis and many more.

Over the years, Overmire's interests have shifted from performing to writing and teaching. A poet at heart, in recent times he has been focusing on education and working on global issues.

Overmire's poetry has been widely published in the U.S. and abroad in hundreds of magazines, journals, and anthologies. *New York Minute* is his fifth collection of poems. The others are *The Ghost of Rabbie Burns: An American Poet's Journey Through Scotland; Honor and Remembrance: A Poetic Journey Through American History; Report From X-Star 10*, a collection of Sci Fi poetry; and *Gone Hollywood*, a reckoning of experiences in the Tinsel Town heart of American media and celebrity.

Overmire is also the author of five genealogy books including *Digging for Ancestral Gold: The Fun and Easy Way to Get Started on Your Genealogy Quest*, as well as two epic family histories: *One Immigrant's Legacy: The Overmyer Family in America, 1751-2009* and *A Revolutionary American Family: The McDonalds of Somerset County, New Jersey*. Having spent much of the last two decades immersed in genealogical and historical research, Overmire has created several genealogical reference databases on the Internet including *The Ancestry of Overmire, Tifft, Richardson, Bradford, Reed*, on Rootsweb, which has received over 1.8 million hits and has helped hundreds of thousands of people trace their family trees and find their connections to famous historical figures.

The book that has drawn the most worldwide attention, however, is a philosophical work titled, *The One Idea That Saves The World: A Call to Conscience and A Call to Action*. Overmire calls it "a blueprint for world peace." It has been praised for its compassionate, common sense approach to many of the world's most pressing issues.

Laurence and his wife Nancy McDonald now live in West Linn, Oregon. Both teach public speaking and arts-related programs through *Oregon Children's Theatre* in Portland and *Lakewood Center for the Arts* in Lake Oswego.

Find out more at laurenceovermire.com

www.ingramcontent.com/pod-product-compliance
Lightning Source LLC
Chambersburg PA
CBHW032044150426
43194CB00006B/417